Estate Planning Success™ for Pennsylvania Residents

"Easy to read, objective. By using this guide and the Estate Planning Team, the reader can have peace of mind knowing their estate plan reflects their own unique desires."

– *Stephen H. Frishberg, Esq. LL.M. (TAX), CPA, Attorney at Law, Blue Bell, PA*

"This is something that has been needed for many years. I am glad Mark finally took the time to put this information in book form, not only for the layperson but also for professionals. It will be a handy reference tool!"

– *Michele J. Garman, CFP, V.P., Senior Trust Advisor, Wachovia Bank, Lancaster, PA*

"Mr. James has done a thorough job of addressing estate planning concerns for Pennsylvania residents. Anyone serious about getting the most value out of the estate planning process should read this handbook!"

– *William B. Henry, J.D., CFP, Edward Jones Investments, Coudersport, PA*

"This book presents the confusing and jargon-filled world of estate planning in a format that makes the information quickly and easily understood, and the benefits easily applied to save you money."

– *Wayne R. Gongaware, LUTCF, FIC, Aid Association for Lutherans, Lititz, PA*

"As an experienced estate planner, I am impressed with the way Mr. James has organized a subject replete with complexity and presented it in a commendably clear and straight forward manner."

– *Steven T. Lees, Esq., CFSC, Trust Officer, Newtown Bank, Newtown, PA*

"The most informational and useful guide on estate planning. James writes from painstaking research and hard-earned experience. There is little he does not cover and cover well. I will be making copies of this book available to my clients to help them through the estate planning process."

– *Scott R. Monger, LUTCF, MDRT, Leola, PA*

"For the Pennsylvania resident, the information contained within is as well organized, as thoroughly comprehensive and as easily understood as any book I have ever reviewed on the subject. Perhaps its greatest strength is the innovative and creative techniques that so skillfully build on the traditional mainstays of the Pennsylvania law."

– *Michael D. Novak, CFP, Master's Financial Associates, Inc., Lancaster, PA*

"This is a unique resource that brings a complex subject…down to a level that is understandable by…everyone. This book is helpful and critically needed."

– *Martyn S. Babitz, Esq., V.P., Senior Estate Planner, PNC Advisors, Philadelphia, PA*

"It will empower you with estate planning options you never knew existed."

– *Charles Bauman, Executive Director, Friendship Community, Lancaster, PA*

"Two groups will find this book of particular value: Pennsylvania consumers who have been looking for a practical and inspiring book to guide them through the estate planning process, and professional advisors looking for a 'primer' on Pennsylvania estate planning."

– *Jack J. Hetherington, Esq., CELA, Attorney at Law Warminster, PA*

"Finally there is one source that covers it all. Thanks for taking the time to write it, because it was long overdue."

– *Charles A. DeBow, Jr., CLU, ChFC, AEP, Dresher, PA*

"I highly recommend it to those looking for a succinct, easy to read guide that makes this entire process much more understandable. I found it very interesting and informative and being the fact that I have been in the advancement field for 22 years, I found the chapter on Charitable Estate Planning of great help for individuals who are contemplating a gift to a charity in our Commonwealth. Great job, really enjoyed it."

– *Gary L. Bukowski, CFRE, Vice President, Institutional Placement, Mercyhurst College, Erie, PA*

"You won't get 'lost' in the subject matter. You will be able to quickly pull out the information that relates to your specific situation to save you time and frustration."

– *Sarah Young Fisher, ChFC, CFP, CFSC, EA, Fisher Advisors, Inc., Mountville, PA, Author,* Complete Idiot's Guide to Personal Finance In Your 40s and 50s

"This book is a very informative compiling of estate planning techniques that every Pennsylvanian should be exposed to and utilize for the implementation of their estate plan."

– *Julian A. Marturano, CLU, ChFC, LUTCF, The MONY Group, Irwin, PA*

"Mark James has written a great reference for the public to be educated and then, hopefully, motivated to preserve their legacies. He has provided Pennsylvanians a balanced approach to the use of wills and revocable living trusts."

– *John J. Schneider, Esq., A.E.P., Attorney at Law, Milford, PA*

"The unique point of view makes the subject matter come to life. The author's 15 years of experience in estate planning sheds light on estate planning solutions in a fast-paced and clear way."

– *David Stork, Esq., Private Wealth Management, Investors Trust Company, Wyomissing, PA*

Estate Planning Success™ for Pennsylvania Residents

by Mark L. James, M.B.A., J.D., LL.M.(tax)

with a Foreword by Michael Geer,
President, Pennsylvania Family Institute

BARRON
PUBLISHING CO.

Barron Publishing Co.
Lancaster, Pennsylvania

For updates on the material in this book, visit www.barronpublishing.com.

Estate Planning Success™ for Pennsylvania Residents

Published by

Barron Publishing Co.
Post Office Box 5039
Lancaster, Pennsylvania 17606
www.barronpublishing.com

"Estate Planning Success™" is a trademark of Barron Publishing Co.

PRINTED IN THE UNITED STATES OF AMERICA

Production Editor: Janice Phelps

Interior Design: Peter Bumpus

Cover Design: George Foster

James, Mark L.

Estate planning success for Pennsylvania residents / Mark L. James -- 1st ed.

p. cm.

includes index

ISBN: 0-9716376-0-1

LCCN: 2002105254

1. Estate planning--Pennsylvania. I. Title

KFP140.Z9J36 2002 346.74805'2

QBI01-201473

To my mother, Jean B. James.

She instilled in me the importance of being devoted to one's faith and family by the way she lived her life — always seeing the silver lining in the dark clouds, always positive, always encouraging and loving. A portion of the sales price of each book is being donated to scholarship funds in her honor at two colleges she attended: Grove City College in Grove City, PA, where she attended from 1939 through 1941, and Mercyhurst College in Erie, PA, where she graduated with a B.A. in 1981. These donations are being made to continue my mother's commitment to education and to make a college education at these excellent institutions available to those who may not be able to afford it.

Warning and Disclaimer

The laws, rules, and regulations applicable to estate planning are highly complex and constantly changing. In addition, accurate information can become outdated overnight as the IRS, U.S. Congress, Pennsylvania legislators and court cases may shift policy. This book is intended to provide a general broad overview regarding estate planning for Pennsylvania residents and to provide suggestions regarding possible estate planning strategies relating to different situations. It is not a substitute for the advice of a qualified professional regarding your specific situation.

This book is designed to provide accurate and authoritative information in regard to the subject matter covered. It is published with the understanding that the publisher, author and contributors are not engaged in rendering legal, accounting or other professional service. If legal advice or other professional advice, including financial, is required, the services of a competent professional person should be sought.

The author, publisher and contributors to this book specifically disclaim any responsibility for any liability, loss, or risk (personal, financial, or otherwise) that may be claimed or incurred as a consequence, directly or indirectly, of the use and/or application of any of the contents of this book.

If you do not wish to be bound by the above, you may return this book to the publisher for a full refund.

A Note about the Glossary

Throughout this book you will see words and phrases in small caps when they are first introduced. These terms are listed in the Glossary, starting on page 235.

Contents at a Glance

Table of Contents

Foreword

In my line of work, which involves a mix of politics, family and faith (two of which you're never supposed to talk about!), I've witnessed first hand the difference between a statesman and an ordinary politician. As it has been said, a statesman is a person who thinks about the next generation; a politician is only thinking about the next election.

Well, to some degree, as individuals and family members we can be measured on a similar scale. Each of us face choices: to plan for the future and to care for those whom we love, or to think only of the next weekend, or the next purchase or the next getaway. Are we acting in a statesmanlike fashion when it comes to managing our own assets – our families, our businesses, our homes?

Pennsylvania's history is replete with examples of those who gave thought to those who would follow in the future. Those who pledged their lives, fortunes and sacred honor at Philadelphia in 1776 were doing so not for themselves, but for the benefit of their country and those they loved.

The framers of our Constitution declared firmly its purposes, among which was to "secure the blessings of liberty to ourselves *and our posterity.*" And even today, Pennsylvania is listed among the top states in the nation for philanthropic giving, led in no small measure by the many significant charitable foundations created by families looking to build a better future for their posterity, and a better society in which they would live. In short, we have a noble heritage here in the Keystone State that should inspire us even more to plan well for the future.

However, Pennsylvania's laws don't always make it easy. For example, here at the Pennsylvania Family Institute, we've been at work over the years to relieve Pennsylvania families of the burden of the state's inheritance tax. It's a tax that has hurt families — our farmers, our small family businesses, those who have worked hard and have something to pass on to their children. The result: Farms that have been in families for generations are forced to use precious cash to pay the tax man. Small businesses that provide livelihoods for many families are placed at risk when the founder dies. And hard-earned nest eggs, set aside for children or grandchildren, are seriously eroded when the government takes its portion.

Thankfully, there's help. In this excellent, informative book Mark L. James draws on his wealth of experience in estate planning and tax law to give Pennsylvania families the tools they need to plan well for the future. In clear, concise and easy-to-digest language, Mark tackles the tough choices on finance and estate issues, enabling even the novice to understand the options and undertake a wise course of action.

Families are the best health, education and welfare institution ever devised, and they need all the help they can get in these days to carry out their all-important mission. I heartily recommend this book for every Pennsylvania family that seeks to do what families do best, and frankly, what no one else will do for them: plan and provide for the future.

– *Michael Geer*
President, Pennsylvania Family Institute
1240 North Mountain Road, Harrisburg, PA 17112
717-545-0600 mail@pafamily.org

Preface

I want to help you avoid the trauma and hard feelings that I have seen many families endure because of the failure to plan. I have seen heirs endure lawsuits brought on because of the decedent's failure to plan. I have seen families devastated when they learn that their loved one was already incompetent and not able to sign a power of attorney to avoid a guardianship hearing. And, I have seen the look on executors' faces as they sign checks made out to the Internal Revenue Service for hundreds of thousands of dollars in payment of the federal estate tax. I have been involved in what goes wrong due to the failure to plan and it is my sincere desire that this book will help you plan your estate to avoid future problems.

The purpose of this book, then, is to present the world of estate planning in the most practical and understandable terms possible. The book is designed to allow you to read specific chapters that pertain to your individual needs. Each chapter addresses particular estate planning strategies related to your stage in life or your needs. Ultimately, of course, you will need assistance from experienced estate planning advisors to work out the options and strategies for your own situation.

This book developed from a series of continuing education lectures that I gave in the mid-1990s to financial planners. During those workshops, I prepared outlines laced with war stories from my experiences in the practical application of estate planning with my clients. Since the preparation of those initial outlines, *Estate Planning Success™ for Pennsylvania Residents* has been researched exhaustively and the contents have been honed into what is intended to be a reference guide for both the estate planner and the estate planner's client.

There are many people without whose help this book would never have happened that I would like to thank. First, I would like to thank Sarah Randolph who spent hundreds of hours typing thousands of pages for the last couple of years. She has learned to not only read my writing but read my mind as well. I would also like to thank Anita Sproles for assisting with innumerable calls, letters, faxes and e-mails related to this project. She did all this while keeping the office running during my "book days." Thanks to Lisa Ebersole who provided me with terrific research capabilities on the Internet. She would have answers for me almost before I hung the phone up asking my question.

J. Marlin Stutzman, my partner, not only provided a large extent of substantive insight, but also kept the office running and the bills paid during the course of writing this book. Thanks, Marlin.

To the members of my technical advisory board, I say thank you for your generous contribution of time and expertise to this project. I am deeply privileged to have had forty-two of the best minds assist me by reading chapters of the original manuscript and offering me new insights and improvements to the text. Each member is listed in the Appendix of this book, and I encourage you to review it to see who these professionals are. Also, Wayne Badorf's enthusiasm for this project has helped spur me on at those times when everything seemed to get bogged down.

Thanks also to my clients. Each one contributed to my learning and my ability to communicate estate planning strategies.

Thank you, family, for your support during this project. Thanks, Heather, Megan and Allison, for being so patient with me and a special thanks to Lindsay for your help with the Glossary.

Janice Phelps, my production editor, of indypub, LLC always exhibited confidence in the book. Her assistance on this project has this book as readable and delightful as it is. I look forward to working with her on future projects in years to come. I am also grateful to Dan Poynter for teaching me how to write a book and get it published. Five years ago I stumbled upon Dan's book, *Is There a Book Inside You?,* and not only did Dan help me discover that there was a book inside me, he also helped me get it out.

PART I

Estate Planning Fundamentals

"Remember: it is not given to man to take his goods with him.
No one goes away and then comes back."

– from the tomb of Egyptian King Inyotef, 2600 B.C.

1

The Estate Planning Process

Topics Include

The Estate Planning Team

Finding an Estate Planning Attorney

Reasonable Fees for an Estate Planning Attorney

An Overview of the Estate Planning Process

Introduction

ESTATE PLANNING: A FORMIDABLE SOUNDING ACTIVITY to many people. Confusing. Time consuming. Fraught with legal jargon and susceptible to the pitches of salespeople. Embroiled with emotion and family loyalties (and disloyalties) and reminding us of our mortality. Something perhaps better left for another day…

If you've taken the first step and purchased this book, then it's clear that you are willing to spend the time necessary to create an estate plan in agreement with your personal wishes. Or, perhaps you have a plan and realize that from time to time it is worthwhile to review.

It is important to note, and certainly motivating to hear, that despite what you might think, you *do* have an estate plan. Or rather, there is a plan in place. The question is, is it your plan or someone else's?

An Estate Plan Is a Responsibility & an Opportunity

Think back to the time when you were starting out in adult life. You may have owned a car, gotten married, had a child. Then, a home was purchased; 401(k)s and IRAs were implemented; perhaps a business was started and assets accumulated. By and by, your estate grew and involved the lives of those you care about and for whom you are responsible. As with each new venture in your life, your assets multiplied, so did the opportunity for an unforeseen event to put everything you worked so hard to accomplish into the hands of a legal system completely unfamiliar with your personal goals and wishes.

An estate plan is a way for your preferences, experience and wisdom to benefit those people and organizations closest to your heart.

An estate plan is your opportunity to clearly define exactly how you want the assets that will endure after you to be distributed and to whom. Also, an estate plan is a way for you to define now, while in good health, what you would like to take place with regard to your care and assets should you become incapacitated. An estate plan is a way for your preferences, experience and wisdom to benefit those people and organizations closest to your heart.

My goal in writing this book is to give you a clear understanding of the steps needed to keep more money, control and peace of mind within your family and to encourage you to begin your plan as soon as possible. ESTATE PLANNING includes the creation, implementation and monitoring of your unique plan to achieve your goals. This book specifically addresses estate planning for residents of Pennsylvania. State inheritance and tax laws vary and also, at times, are revised. Therefore, this book is not meant to be a substitute for legal advice, but a tool for you to use in formulating your plan.

Before a plan is created, you will need to assemble an estate planning team.

Your Estate Planning Team

Most people will agree that their estate planning goals include providing for their spouse and/or minor children and minimizing inheritance taxes. Additionally, there are individual goals that differ from one person to another, such as providing long-term care for an adult child with special needs, ensuring care for oneself or one's spouse should they become incapacitated, passing the family business or farm onto an heir, or bequeathing assets to a charity.

Hiring qualified professionals is absolutely crucial to the clarity, cohesiveness and feasibility of your plan.

Whatever your personal goals in regard to your estate plan, hiring qualified professionals is absolutely crucial to the clarity, cohesiveness and feasibility of your plan. You and your heirs will benefit from working with an estate planning team by keeping more money and control within your family.

Rapid changes in the area of estate planning are occurring. It is no longer sufficient to simply have an attorney prepare a WILL or invest solely in ANNUITIES "to avoid probate." As you will learn in this book, the challenges of estate planning are surmountable, but it requires a professional team to create a plan that will meet your goals. Take a moment to look at the various professionals that might form your team. Not everyone's estate planning team will consist of all team members listed on the following page. Indeed, most estate plans are established using only the input of two or three members of the team.

The Estate Planning Team

Accountant

Your accountant is an essential member of the team to prepare tax returns, handle valuation issues, and assist with integrating business planning and estate planning.

Life Insurance Agent

This professional will assist you with the planning and use of life insurance in estate planning. In addition, the life insurance agent is needed to keep you advised of the status of your insurance policies, recommending any changes based on your changing needs. It is critical that your life insurance policies have the correct beneficiary designations.

Financial Planners, Investment Advisors & Trust Officers

These advisors are also helpful to have on the team. They can provide needed insight regarding the correct investments, their allocation and registration. They will also assist you in considering whether a corporate trustee will be helpful for your needs.

Estate Planning Attorney

This attorney will assist with designing the plan and will prepare the necessary legal documents and confirm that they are properly signed.

Planned Giving Officer

This person is considered a relatively new addition to estate planning teams, and would be from one of your favorite charities. These professionals also go by the title of director of planned gifts or director of development. The planned giving officer is well versed in the areas of charitable estate planning and can give you creative ideas that will maximize your charitable giving and help you achieve your estate planning goals.

What an Experienced Estate Planning Team Brings to the Table

Experienced estate planning professionals protect your ASSETS by seeing the big picture. For example, several years ago I had a business client see me to review his estate plan. He had a will he prepared using a legal software package. I reviewed the will for him, and, yes, it was technically correct.

My client explained that he had just purchased a $1 million life insurance contract and wanted to name his children as the beneficiaries of the life insurance. The will contained trusts for his children, so they would not receive their inheritance until they were thirty years old. Unfortunately, the life insurance contract listed the children as the beneficiaries rather than the trust. If the documents had been left as this conscientious father had originally signed them, the children — if their father had died before them — would have received their entire benefits at age eighteen. The life insurance proceeds would not have been controlled by the will. Although his will was correct, it did not reflect his personal wishes.

No two estate plans can be identical, because no two people are identical.

When choosing the members of your estate planning team, the most important consideration is that before your estate plan is designed a face-to-face meeting takes place between you and the team members who will help you design your plan. No two estate plans can be identical, because no two people are identical. Individual situations vary based on the amount and complexity of assets people own as well as different goals. To be successful, your estate plan must reflect your personal values, desires and goals. Therefore, your meeting with estate planning professionals before your plan is designed is critical.

Finding an Estate Planning Attorney

In Pennsylvania, there is currently no certification available that permits qualified attorneys to identify themselves as specialists in estate

Yellow Page ads that list attorneys under "Areas of Practice" can be misleading.

planning law. It is interesting to note that in Pennsylvania there are approximately 22,000 attorneys actively engaged in private practice. Of this total, only 225 are certified in *any* specialty. Yellow Page ads that list attorneys under "Areas of Practice" can be misleading, because there is no prerequisite necessary for an attorney to list his name under these specialized areas of the law. Since an attorney cannot hold himself out as a specialist in estate planning law, what factors might indicate that an attorney may be knowledgeable in estate planning?*

EXPERIENCE

It is important to find an attorney knowledgeable in the areas of income tax, estate tax, and Pennsylvania's inheritance tax. You will need to determine: Is the attorney experienced in writing TRUSTS? Also, is he knowledgeable regarding taxes?

EDUCATION

Has the attorney taken continuing legal education courses related to estate planning? In addition, there is an advanced degree some attorneys achieve called a master of laws (LL.M.). A master of laws degree is awarded to an attorney who completes a post-graduate course of study in advanced areas of the law. An LL.M. in taxation would indicate one's familiarity with the tax issues relating to estate planning.

An attorney's membership in certain professional associations would indicate an interest in estate planning.

PROFESSIONAL ASSOCIATIONS

One national association of experienced estate planning attorneys is known as the American College of Trust and Estate Council (ACTEC). This is an association of several thousand attorneys and law professors who have at least ten years of practice in probate, trust law and estate planning. The American College of Trust and Estate Council can be contacted at 3415 S. Sepulveda Blvd., Suite 330, Los Angeles, CA, 90034. Telephone: (310) 398-1888. www.actec.org.

Another professional association is the National Association of Estate Planners and Councils. This organization offers two professional

* Certainly both men and women equally fill the professional requirements necessary to assist the reader in reaching estate planning goals. My use of the male pronoun is to simplify the reading of this text and in no way implies a preference of one gender over another when choosing one's team.

designations. One is the Accredited Estate Planner (**AEP**) and the other is the Estate Planning Law Specialist. (The latter is not recognized in Pennsylvania as a board-certified speciality as of the publication of this book.) To locate attorneys in Pennsylvania who have received these designations, you can contact the National Association of Estate Planners and Councils at 270 S. Bryn Mawr Ave., Bryn Mawr, PA, 19010. Telephone: (610) 526-1389. www.naepc.org

A third national professional association is the National Academy of Elder Law Attorneys, Inc. (NAELA). Membership in the academy is open to licensed attorneys who are practicing in the area of elder law or who are interested in legal issues pertaining to the elderly.

The National Academy of Elder Law Attorneys is a professional association of attorneys concerned with improving the availability and delivery of legal services to older persons. With the emergence of elder law as an acknowledged area of practice, NAELA is striving to define the area of practice, establish standards, and create an information network among elder law attorneys. Through NAELA, attorneys exchange ideas and information on substantive elder law issues and the development of an elder law practice. The academy was formed in 1987 and currently has more than 3000 members in fifty states.

> For additional information on NAELA, contact NAELA, 1604 N. Country Club, Tucson, AZ, 85716, or call (520) 881-4005. www.naela.org

You can determine an attorney's participation in the above associations by asking him directly, reviewing literature sent by his office, or by reviewing the corresponding associations' membership lists, which can usually be found in local libraries or in the law library of your county courthouse. Referrals from other professionals, such as your accountant, financial planner, or insurance agent, might be a good place to start.

Once you have the name of an attorney qualified to be a part of your estate planning team, it is important to talk briefly with him over the phone and, if you feel comfortable with this initial conversation, arrange the first meeting face-to-face in his office. At that time you can review your personal estate planning goals and ask questions regarding estimated fees for legal assistance.

The First Meeting with Your Attorney

INITIAL CONSULTATION COSTS

As far as the fee you might incur for a first meeting, attorneys generally handle initial consultations one of three ways:

1. Some attorneys have no fee for the initial consultation. If you choose not to engage the attorney's services after the consultation, it has cost you nothing.
2. The second method attorneys use to charge for the initial consultation is a fixed fee. This could be $75.00 to $100.00 or more for the initial consultation. Some attorneys waive the initial consultation fee if you choose them to do your work.
3. The third way attorneys charge is by requiring a small amount, such as $50.00 to $75.00, for the first thirty minutes, and the attorney bills his hourly rate thereafter.

THE ESTATE PLANNING QUESTIONNAIRE

Let's assume that you've obtained the name of an attorney who specializes in estate planning and is knowledgeable about tax laws. He also participates in professional associations related to estate planning. You've called the office, had a good initial conversation and set up an appointment time to explore a working relationship. At this point, the attorney's office should mail you a questionnaire prior to your office visit. This Estate Planning Questionnaire will save you time and money. Completing the form is the first important step in planning your estate. (*See Appendix 1 for a sample form.*)

The Estate Planning Questionnaire will save you time and money.

In preparation for your initial meeting, you should bring the completed questionnaire. This will give the attorney a good understanding of your family situation as well as the size and complexity of your estate and an initial view of your goals. Also, you will want to bring a copy of the DEEDS to any real estate you own and BENEFICIARY designations of your life insurance, IRA, or qualified retirement plans.

If you have been working with another professional advisor, such as an accountant, on your estate planning, it is appropriate to have them accompany you to your meeting with the attorney, if you so desire.

Keep in mind that the purpose of this first meeting is to describe your specific situation and determine the attorney's recommendations to help you achieve your goals. Another objective of the initial meeting is to

The Initial Phone Call to the Attorney's Office

When calling the attorney's office for the first time, you will probably speak with a secretary or assistant. Ask to speak with the attorney. If you cannot speak with the attorney on the first call, leave a message for him to call you back. If you do not hear back, then he may not be the best attorney for your team.

During your initial phone conversation, ask a few questions such as:

- "Do you charge for the initial consultation?"
- "Do you prepare trusts?"
- "Do you do federal estate tax planning?" and,
- "How do you charge for your services?"

If you are satisfied with your telephone conversation and agree with any charge you might incur for an initial consultation, then set an appointment. If not, then simply say "thank you" and end the conversation.

The answers to these questions will be much more revealing than merely asking "How much do you charge for a will?" As I'll explain later on, there is much more to planning your estate than simply creating a will.

(If you prefer not to speak with an attorney by phone before your initial appointment or if the attorney cannot speak with you, you will have the opportunity to learn about him and his services and fees at the initial meeting.)

determine what legal fees will be incurred if the attorney fulfills the recommendations he has made. It is also a good idea to have the attorney tell you how long it will take to complete the necessary documents.

Keep in mind that the purpose of this first meeting is to describe your specific situation and determine the attorney's recommendations to help you achieve your goals.

Let's assume that this first meeting goes well and, at some point during the discussion, you decide to hire the attorney. Schedule the next meeting before leaving his office. Also, you might want to ask that the attorney have all documents prepared for you to review at your next meeting, and, if they are acceptable to you, you could then sign the documents at the second meeting. This second meeting should generally be two to three weeks after the initial meeting and should last from forty-five minutes to two hours depending on the complexity of your documents.

If you feel that you would prefer to review drafts of your documents and discuss them with other advisors before returning to the attorney's office to sign them, simply ask the attorney to send you drafts for your review and/or the review of your other professional advisors.

Of course, a first meeting might not yield enough information for the attorney to create the necessary documents, or there may be issues that need to be discussed with your spouse, children, or your accountant or insurance agent. It is not unusual to need more than one visit as more time may be needed to think and review the options discussed. If this is the case, simply tell the attorney that you would like to take more time for reflection or schedule a second meeting for further review.

What Are Reasonable Fees for an Estate Planning Attorney?

You've located an experienced attorney, talked on the phone, met in his office and are ready to move forward. What would be considered reasonable fees for his services? How much should you expect to pay for your estate planning documents?

This question is like asking how much a car should cost. Is it a new car? Is it a used car? Is it a Yugo? Is it a Cadillac? There are so many variables that it is not possible to specify what a reasonable fee for legal

The lowest fee should not be the only criteria for choosing an attorney.

services rendered should be. You will need to do some research pertinent to your individual situation. The best approach is to ask two or three attorneys to give you an estimate of their fees. Then you will have an idea of the range of legal fees related to the preparation of the estate plan. Always keep in mind that the lowest fee should not be the only criteria for choosing an estate planning attorney.

Most attorneys base their fees on one of the three billing arrangements noted below. The billing arrangement should be clearly communicated to you prior to the onset of your legal work.

Billing Arrangements

Fixed Fee (Also Known as Established Fee)

Under the fixed fee approach, an attorney will quote you a fixed fee to do the work he is engaged to do.

Quoting an Estimated Range of Fees

It is difficult for attorneys to charge a fixed fee for complex services. This is because every case is different and the attorney is never completely sure what work he will get into. For this reason, many attorneys quote an estimated range of fees.

Hourly Billing

Some attorneys will simply charge by the hour at an agreed-upon rate for the time spent working on your estate plan.

An Overview of the Estate Planning Process

The process of planning your estate is one that entails many considerations, discussions and assessments of what is important to you and your heirs, your community, and your favorite charitable organizations.

There is no question but that the process requires careful discussion and consideration of these factors. For some, this process will entail nothing more than determining whom they would name as guardians of their minor children. For others, with more complex estates, there will be many more considerations.

It is helpful to separate the estate planning process into six phases. The time necessary to proceed through all six of these phases can be as short as two or three weeks or as long as two or three years, depending upon your specific situation. The following explanation of the estate planning process is not a rigid outline, but is intended to provide an overview. Let's start with Phase One...

Phase One: Gather the Required Information

Gathering your documents together is the first step in creating your comprehensive plan.

Gathering your documents together for your team to review is the first step in creating your comprehensive plan. Completing the Estate Planning Questionnaire mentioned earlier in this chapter is also part of the first step. You will use the questionnaire to define and specify the rest of the information you will need.

Family Information

These are the people who will be affected by your planning. This includes family members, as well as other people who you desire to receive (or not receive!) a portion of your estate. Be sure to include their names, addresses, birthdays, and social security numbers.

Financial Information

Accurate financial information is critical to the estate plan. It is important to have an inventory listing your assets and LIABILITIES. In addition to listing the current value of your assets, it is also important to confirm how they are TITLED. Other information needed includes life insurance policies and retirement plan benefits.

Establish Your Goals & Put Them in Writing

Your estate plan is as individual as your family. Nevertheless, typical goals might be:

- Confirm that your assets reach the people and charities you choose while avoiding family conflict over your estate.
- Minimize your estate's losses to taxes, excess legal fees and expenses and avoid forced sale of assets to pay these costs.
- Keep control over assets "from the grave" and prevent heirs from squandering their inheritance.

The Six Phases of Estate Planning:
1. Gather
2. Estimate
3. Design
4. Implement
5. Calculate Again
6. Monitor

Name Those Who Will Carry Out Your Wishes

You will need to consider who you wish to serve as the executor to settle your estate. In addition, if you are preparing any trusts in your plan, you will want to begin thinking about who you would appoint to serve as TRUSTEE. If you have minor children, you should name a GUARDIAN to care for them. Lastly, regarding possible incapacity, it would be important to consider who should serve as the agent in your POWER OF ATTORNEY, and your LIVING WILL.

PHASE TWO: ESTIMATE TAXES & EXPENSES DUE UNDER YOUR EXISTING ESTATE PLAN

As mentioned earlier, whether you've created one or not, an estate plan is in place with regard to your assets. Unfortunately, the court's plan may not be identical to your wishes. Before implementing your plan, it is helpful to calculate the taxes and expenses that would be payable from your estate (and your surviving spouse's estate) at death under your existing plan. It is also important to determine the LIQUID ASSETS available to pay these last expenses and taxes.

PHASE THREE: DESIGN A NEW ESTATE PLAN

The third step in the process is to design an estate plan to accomplish your unique goals and objectives at the least cost.

PHASE FOUR: IMPLEMENT THE PLAN

After you and your estate planning team have reviewed and agreed upon your estate plan, the plan should be implemented. This includes your attorney's preparing and drafting of the documents necessary. Additional steps would be acquiring life insurance or long-term care insurance, if necessary, and the re-registration of assets and changing the beneficiary designation on IRAs, qualified retirement plans and life insurance. Gifts to charity should be thoroughly discussed as they offer many benefits to a good estate plan. All of this activity would occur using the services of the members of your estate planning team.

PHASE FIVE: MAKE A SECOND CALCULATION OF TAXES & EXPENSES

After the plan has been designed and implemented, it is important to make a second calculation of taxes and expenses payable from your estate at death. The savings in taxes and expenses will give you a sense of accomplishment and peace of mind that the plan has been implemented to reflect your concerns and protect your estate.

PHASE SIX: MONITOR YOUR ESTATE PLAN

Change is constant in tax law and laws regarding wills and trusts.

In addition to changes in taxes and laws, families are in a constant state of flux with regard to relationships, marriages, deaths or adoptions and personal income or the value of assets. For this reason, it is important to monitor your estate plan. The plan should be reviewed every two to three years in light of the changes in your life as well as the changes in laws and taxation. You may want to get in the habit of checking to see if your plan needs brought up to date each fall when planning personal and professional goals for the coming year.

Summary

Like many worthwhile activities, estate planning is a process and not an event. The process begins by retaining an attorney with experience in trusts and tax laws. Your preparation in defining estate planning goals and assembling other important team members, such as an accountant and life insurance agent, will ensure a smooth process. Never underestimate the importance of face-to-face meetings with your team and establish a set time every two or three years to monitor your plan and keep it up to date.

2

Estate Planning Fundamentals in Pennsylvania

Topics Include

A Comprehensive Approach to Estate Planning

The Three Forms of Joint Ownership

Non-Probate Assets and Who Pays the Taxes

Post-Mortem Estate Planning: Electing Against the Will & Disclaimers

Introduction

IT IS HUMAN NATURE to avoid tasks that are confusing and seem complex, especially where money and family are involved. Plus, there are a lot of things we would rather do — clean the garage, work in the yard, repaint the living room — than give serious thought to what should happen to our estate after we die. Few people are comfortable spending concentrated effort thinking about their mortality.

Neither are we eager to envision ourselves mentally or physically incapacitated. Still, reality exists, time marches on, and we must do our best with that over which we can exercise some control. Planning our estate is one aspect where we can demonstrate forethought, consideration, and financial wisdom for the people and organizations we care about the most.

Planning our estate is one aspect where we can demonstrate forethought, consideration, and financial wisdom.

Some of the confusion and mystery that surround the world of estate planning can be attributed to attacking the plan in a piecemeal manner. Many discussions neglect a holistic approach, an overall plan. For instance, we might think about designating the beneficiary of our life insurance policy when we are sitting with our insurance agent. We think about inheritance taxes when we are talking with our lawyer or accountant. Appropriate, trustworthy family members or business associates come to mind when setting up business or personal bank accounts. A piecemeal approach is like having someone explain the particular moves of the chess pieces without ever explaining the various strategies of chess. The purpose of this chapter is to lay the groundwork regarding the fundamentals of estate planning in Pennsylvania and approach the estate planning process with an understanding of how various parts of the plan relate to one another. In this way we can develop an overall strategy that meets your goals.

We will discuss how assets pass at death, the probate process in Pennsylvania, DISCLAIMERS, and spousal elections. It is important to gain a clear understanding of the fundamentals so that you can incorporate the material in later chapters within the broader picture of your personal estate plan.

What Is Estate Planning?

The definition of the phrase "estate planning" may seem to vary according to the profession of the person doing the talking. An attorney, for example, would say that estate planning is the preparation of wills and trusts to memorialize the client's wishes. An accountant might state that estate planning is arranging your affairs to minimize taxes. A life insurance agent might define estate planning as purchasing life insurance. All would be correct, yet they would have only a piece of the overall plan.

Your estate is the total value of all assets that you own.

Before answering the question "What is estate planning?" we must clarify "What is your estate *for planning purposes?*" In other words, how do we define your estate? We will define your estate as the *total value* of all assets that you own. This includes assets held solely in your name, such as bank accounts and automobile titles, as well as assets owned jointly with others, such as your home or savings accounts. Even your life insurance, IRAs and retirement plan benefits are a part of your estate. Estate *planning,* then, is formulating specific plans for the management of your assets during your lifetime in the event that you become incapacitated. It is also planning for the distribution of your assets to others upon your death.

To emphasize the holistic approach, the preceding definitions are very broad. Since this book covers such a wide range of subjects, the depth of any particular topic area may be limited. You should inquire with your team members (i.e. accountant, estate planning attorney, life insurance agent, etc.) about any specific questions pertaining to your estate. You might want to start a list of questions that come up as you read through this book. The objective of *Estate Planning Success™ for Pennsylvania Residents* is to describe the essential areas of estate planning so that you have an opportunity to consider the breadth of options available to you and to give you peace of mind knowing that you have considered all of the important issues.

The Estate Planning Revolution

The business of estate planning is rapidly changing. Pennsylvania's residents, like all baby boomers throughout the U.S., are approaching midlife and retirement. The number of residents within this age group is expanding. The 2000 census revealed that that are over 4.75 million Pennsylvanians aged 45 and older. As this segment of the population ages, it becomes important to plan for possible incapacity as well as death.

Another reason the field of estate planning is changing is a significant increase in what are called will substitutes. Until recently, a will was

Your will may provide for a much smaller distribution of your assets than you realize.

all that was needed to transfer one's assets to others after death. Today, however, the importance of the will has been diminished due to the significant growth of will substitutes. A will substitute is a provision established during one's lifetime for the distribution of assets after death. This bypasses the PROBATE process. A common will substitute is the REVOCABLE LIVING TRUST. Other examples are annuities and life insurance. When purchasing an annuity or life insurance policy, the investor names a beneficiary so that on the death of the ANNUITY owner or the insured, the money goes directly to the named beneficiary. *It is not controlled by the will.* Additional will substitutes are IRAs and other retirement plans which name the beneficiaries who are to receive funds upon the death of the owner.

Pennsylvania law enables transfer on death (also known as T.O.D.) arrangements to be made with mutual funds, investment accounts and bank accounts. When registering investment accounts, the investor can make arrangements with the mutual fund, investment company or bank to provide that the investments will be transferred directly to the named beneficiary on the investor's death. As in the previous examples, a T.O.D. account avoids the probate process and passes financial assets to others outside of the will.

It could be argued that creating a plan that does not carry out your wishes may be worse than no plan at all.

What does all this mean for your estate? It means that your will may provide for the distribution of a much smaller portion of your assets than you realize. Yet, ironically, you may have spent more time and attention on your will than on any other part of your estate plan.

Sometimes professional advisors (who were not involved in planning the will or living trust) assist their clients with annuities and T.O.D. accounts to "avoid probate." Probate may be avoided, but the *central coordination* of the estate plan is also bypassed often resulting in assets not going where the original owner intended. To insure that your estate plan is implemented upon your death or incapacity, you will need to be aware of two major problems caused by improper, or piecemeal, planning: a lack of coordination of beneficiaries and confusion regarding who must pay the inheritance and estate taxes.

LACK OF COORDINATION OF BENEFICIARIES

With beneficiary designations playing such an important role in the estate planning process (many people own annuities, life insurance and IRAs), it is important that the provision for the post-death distribution of all your assets reflects your wishes as far as the beneficiaries are concerned.

Many heirs are surprised to discover that certain family members receive significantly larger portions of the estate of a deceased parent than others do. This may not be what the decedent intended, but a result of a lack of planning with regard to beneficiary designations. The right hand must know what the left hand is doing or, in the case of your estate, more likely several right and left hands.

> If you want your son to receive two thirds of a life insurance benefit and your daughter to receive one third along with your collection of antique pottery, it must be spelled out properly within your estate plan. On the other hand, if you want your daughter and son to equally split your entire estate, it is not sufficient to only state so in your will. The life insurance beneficiary should also name both children. If only your son is named as beneficiary, sibling confusion and disappointment are sure to follow.

DETERMINING WHO MUST PAY THE INHERITANCE & ESTATE TAXES

The second issue —Who must pay the INHERITANCE TAX? — is a growing concern. As mentioned earlier, quite often an individual's will states that any taxes due from their estate should be paid from the "probate estate as an expense of administration." (The probate estate is the one portion of your total estate that is controlled by your will.) The assets that we have been discussing (i.e., annuities, life insurance, T.O.D. accounts) all pass outside the will and are known as NON-PROBATE ASSETS. If your will specifies that all taxes are to be paid from your probate estate as an expense of administration, then any inheritance tax due upon

Let us consider the estate of married businessman Jason White.* Mr. White's assets consisted of the family home (which was paid for and held solely in his name), a sizeable annuity, several IRAs and a classic car collection that was his pride and joy. Unfortunately, White developed a passion for ultra-light planes late in life, and one day met an untimely end.

Several years prior to this, White had his attorney create a will. His will stated that all inheritance and estate taxes were to be paid from the probate estate as "an expense of administration." This was in small print; White had read it quickly without much comprehension. He had other things to do, and, "After all, isn't that why I hired a lawyer?" It was definitely his intention that Mrs. White would become the sole owner of the house, their checking and savings accounts, and his IRAs. He assumed that upon his death she would sell the home and move into something smaller, investing the difference and living off the interest. In fact, he'd mentioned this to her a few times.

Mr. White was also concerned about providing an ongoing income for his niece, Mary, who was disabled and unable to earn a sufficient income on her own. Therefore, he designated Mary as the beneficiary of a $100,000 annuity. Mr. and Mrs. White had a son together, Todd. Todd was a successful entrepreneur and did not need financial assistance. He loved Dad's car collection though, and it was left to him.

Through lack of planning, though not lack of concern, Mr. White's estate was handled just as he had specified, although the end result was not in accordance with what he would have wanted. Mrs. White did inherit the house, their joint checking and savings accounts, and the IRAs. Mr. White's niece, Mary, inherited the $100,000 annuity, and his son, Todd, inherited the car collection, which was appraised at $100,000.

What Mr. White did not anticipate, however, was that his probate estate would be responsible for paying the inheritance tax on both Mary's annuity and Todd's car collection. The taxes on these amounts totaled $19,500 (Mary's annuity was taxed at 15% and Todd's car collection was taxed at 4.5%). As the surviving spouse, Mrs. White was not required to pay inheritance tax on what she received from her husband's estate. Unfortunately, since she was the sole heir named in his will, due to the tax language in the will she ended up with $19,500 less than Mr. White intended. Mary never got along with her aunt and chose not to contribute anything toward the $15,000 taxes due on the annuity she received. Fortunately, Todd was willing to sell a car to help his mother with the taxes, but this was not what his dad had intended.

* Examples used throughout this book are hypothetical. Any resemblance to actual people is coincidental.

annuities and IRAs received by your heirs will be paid from the portion of your estate going to the heirs under your will. As a result, those receiving the distribution as a non-probate asset are not required to pay the inheritance tax on the portion of the total estate that they inherit. The residual beneficiaries of the will would have this tax deducted from *their* inheritance.

Incorrect use of tax language in wills contributes to confusion and conflict.

It is not unusual for the beneficiaries under a will to be surprised to discover that non-probate assets have been distributed to someone else. This can result in anything from mild annoyance to angry disagreements to definite hardship on the part of the beneficiary of the will. The incorrect use of tax language in wills contributes to confusion and conflict. This is especially the case when the estate has a substantial amount of non-probate assets that pass to the beneficiaries, while those who receive their inheritance under the will are saddled with paying the full amount of tax on the non-probate assets.

The bottom line of the whole estate planning revolution is that now, more than ever, you need a team to assist you with your estate plan. The team approach provides you with the best planning scenario, because each team member is an expert in their respective field. By working together, your professional advisors can give you the most beneficial plan and ensure that what you want to have happen with your estate is *exactly what happens* when you are no longer around to specify.

What Happens to Your Assets Depends upon "How" You Own Them

ASSETS IN YOUR SOLE NAME (PROBATE ASSETS)

Upon death, assets you owned in your name alone are called PROBATE ASSETS. In a strict sense, probate refers to the legal process that affects such assets. Probate as understood by most people, however, refers to the estate settlement process. This includes probating the will as well as paying taxes and filing papers with the court.

Estate settlement is the process of changing the title of assets from the name of the deceased into the name of the appropriate heir.

Estate settlement, with regard to probate assets, is the process of changing the title of assets from the name of a deceased person into the name of the appropriate heir. It requires notifying both family members and the public that one has died, confirming that the rightful owners receive their inheritance and giving creditors of the decedent an opportunity to present their bills for payment. This process is undertaken by the decedent's executor, and there are fees incurred by the estate to complete this process. Attorney's fees and executor's commissions in Pennsylvania, with respect to settling an estate, are not specified by law but only limited to that which is "reasonable." No specific percentage or fixed fee is defined. Many attorneys follow a fee schedule issued in the 1980s by the Pennsylvania Attorney General's office and based on a percentage of the value of the estate. Other attorneys bill for their services on an hourly basis.

The time required to settle an estate is based on a number of factors including the size of the estate, the complexity of the assets, and family harmony, or lack of it. An average time frame to settle a medium-sized estate would be six to twelve months. If you die with a will, you are known as a TESTATOR. When someone dies without a will, they are said to have died INTESTATE.

Probate Assets

A person's probate estate is made up of only those assets that must go through the probate process before they can be distributed to the heirs. Probate assets include property that is:

- owned solely by the decedent;
- owned jointly with others as tenants in common; and
- life insurance, annuitites, IRAs, and other assets that have no named beneficiary or that name the decedent's estate.

Who Gets What When Someone Dies without a Will

Married Individuals

If you have a husband or wife who survives you and you have no children and your parents are not living, then your spouse would inherit your entire estate. If you have no children, but one or more parents, then your spouse gets the first $30,000.00 and half of the balance. Your surviving parents get the remaining half.

Married with Children

If you and your surviving spouse have children, your spouse gets the first $30,000.00 and half of the balance. The children get equal shares of the remaining half.

If you and your spouse have children and you also have children who are not from your marriage with your spouse, your spouse gets half of your estate and all of your children get equal shares of the other half.

Estates of Single Individuals

If you have any children, each would get equal shares of your estate. Otherwise, your estate would go to the persons who are living at your death in this order of priority:

- your parents;
- your brothers and sisters, or their children;
- your grandparents;
- your uncles and aunts or their descendants; and
- the Commonwealth of Pennsylvania.

Assets Owned Jointly with Others (Non-Probate Assets)

What about assets that you own with others; are they controlled by your will? The distribution of assets that you own jointly with others is *not* controlled by your will. These assets will be controlled BY OPERATION OF LAW. This means that upon your death, your jointly owned assets will *automatically and instantly* belong to those who jointly own them. It cannot be emphasized enough that whether assets are owned jointly between spouses or non-spouses, the distribution of such assets upon death *will not be controlled by your will.* This is important to remember since the work done in your will or living trust would be worthless if all of the assets were owned jointly.

There are three ways two or more people can own the same assets at the same time in Pennsylvania: JOINT TENANTS WITH RIGHTS OF SURVIVORSHIP, TENANTS BY THE ENTIRETIES, and TENANTS IN COMMON.

Non-Probate Assets

Non-probate assets are identified by how they are titled and consist of all assets that are not probate assets, such as:

- assets held jointly with others as joint tenants with rights of survivorship or tenants by the entirety;
- assets payable to a named beneficiary (life insurance, annuity, IRAs, for example); and
- assets promised to others by written agreement (partnership agreement or shareholder's agreement, for example).

Joint Tenants with Rights of Survivorship

This form of joint ownership specifies that when one asset owner dies, the surviving owners automatically receive the deceased owner's share. Assets owned in this manner are typically owned by non-spouses. One disadvantage is that this joint tenancy can be broken by only one joint owner who can sell their interest.

Jointly Owned Property Woes (or "Johnny, buy a tent.")

If I owned a hunting cabin in Potter County as joint tenants with rights of survivorship with my brother, and my will stated that at my death I wanted my interest in the cabin to go to my son, Johnny, this joint tenancy would overrule my will. Regardless of what I stated in my will, my interest in this property would automatically belong to my brother at my death. Johnny would need to buy a tent.

Tenants by the Entireties

Assets held jointly by a husband and wife are known as tenants by the entireties. This means that each has an undivided interest in the whole and that neither the husband nor the wife alone can sell or transfer the asset. It can only be transferred by *both* spouses.

Tenants in Common

There is one form of joint ownership that is indeed controlled by your will. This form of ownership means that when one owner dies, his or her share of the joint asset will remain a part of the estate and go to his or her heirs under the will. If, in the above example, the deed to the cabin stated it was held as tenants in common, then upon my death my

Mother & Daughter Tale of Joint Ownership

Mother Martin is eighty years old and has lived in the family home for sixty years. Her husband passed away many years ago. The Martins had one daughter, Elizabeth. Mother wants Elizabeth to inherit the family home when she dies. To smooth this transition, Mother made Elizabeth a joint owner in the home. At Mother's death, the house will pass to Elizabeth free of the probate process. The creation of the joint ownership, however, was a taxable gift from Mrs. Martin to her daughter. No tax may be due, but if the value of the gift exceeds $11,000, a federal gift tax return will be required. In addition, if mother passes away within one year, only $3,000 in value will escape Pennsylvania inheritance tax.

son, Johnny, would become joint owner of the cabin with my brother, as I had intended.

If a parent places a home in joint ownership with an adult child, and the adult child goes bankrupt, the bankruptcy creditors could force a sale of the home.

One disadvantage with jointly owned assets is the fact that the creditors of any one of the joint owners can attach the asset to the extent of the owner's interest therein. (This is not true for tenants by the entirety assets.) Another disadvantage with joint ownership is that the creation of a joint interest may be a taxable gift.

It is not uncommon for parents to name an adult child as co-owner of their home or a bank account. They may wish to avoid probate or simply want to make it easier to have their child help with managing checking and savings accounts. Yet, if the unfortunate situation were to occur where the child died before the parent, the parent might be faced with having to pay 4.5% INHERITANCE TAX on one-half the value of the asset in order to reclaim total ownership of the property.

Another disadvantage to jointly owned assets is ACCIDENTAL DISINHERITANCE. This can happen when assets are jointly owned, and the law contradicts what is intended in the will. Accidental disinheritance is another reason why it is so important to coordinate all aspects of your estate plan with knowledgeable professionals.

Accidental Disinheritance Woes

Mr. and Mrs. Smith are married and Mrs. Smith dies. Mr. Smith, who manages a large farm that has been in his family for many years, eventually remarries and re-titles the farm into joint names with himself and his second wife. Smith's will has been in place for some time, specifying that upon his death all of his assets will pass on to his children from his first marriage. He has a life insurance policy designating the new Mrs. Smith as beneficiary, so he feels she will be well taken care of and the farm can stay in the family. Unbeknownst to Smith, however, is that even if his will gives everything to his children, upon his death the farm would automatically be owned by his current wife, because the farm deed lists Mr. Smith and this wife as joint owners.

ASSETS GIVEN TO OTHERS BY BENEFICIARY DESIGNATION OR AGREEMENTS (NON-PROBATE ASSETS)

Non-probate assets are not controlled by your will. Annuities, retirement plans, IRAs, SHAREHOLDER AGREEMENTS and partnership agreements are all examples of non-probate assets. Life insurance policies are also non-probate assets. Non-probate assets are distributed to the designated beneficiary regardless of what the will states.

Non-probate assets will be distributed to the designated beneficiary regardless of what your will states.

When you purchase a life insurance policy, you are asked to name a beneficiary to receive the benefits of the policy upon your death. *Regardless of what your will says,* the proceeds will be paid directly to the beneficiaries you named in the life insurance contract. This is why it is important to co-ordinate your will with your life insurance.

The precise wording of beneficiary designation forms is important for a well-planned estate. Preprinted forms may not permit the precise wishes of the insured, so always confirm with both your insurance agent and your estate planning attorney exactly what you want to have happen with regard to life insurance benefits. Life and the circumstances of your family may change over time, and you should periodically review beneficiary forms to confirm their continued accuracy. What seemed appropriate ten, or even five years ago, may not be appropriate today.

Who, What & When

Howard knows that if he dies unexpectedly, his estate will leave a substantial inheritance to his minor children. Therefore, his will states that the children are not to receive their inheritance until they reach age twenty-five. It will also be essential that Howard does not designate as his life insurance beneficiary "my children." He will need to designate the trust in his will as the beneficiary, since the trust defines "the who, what, and when" of these assets and the timing of their transfer to the children. This is because the life insurance is not controlled by the will, and if the beneficiary simply said "my children," they would receive their entire inheritance at age eighteen.

Why Comprehensive Estate Planning Is Important

Since there are three different forms of ownership that control how your assets are distributed at death, it is important to review beneficiary designations and security registrations as well as deeds and other accounts to confirm how each is titled. Also, the exact title of your assets will have an impact on the creditors' rights against your assets.

It is easy to see that even in spite of your well-meaning efforts, as things stand now your estate may not be distributed as you intend. In fact, you may think you do not even have an estate plan, but you *do* have

When To Review Your Estate Plan, Including Wills, Deeds, Insurance Policies & Annuities

- Marriage (Your own or another family member's)
- Retirement planning
- Divorce
- Relocating to Pennsylvania from another state
- A death in the family
- Remarriage
- The birth of a child
- An adoption
- Disability or prolonged illness in the family
- Children reaching adulthood
- A significant increase or reduction in assets
- Selling real estate
- Purchasing real estate
- Purchasing life insurance
- Starting or disbanding a business
- An inheritance from a parent or grandparent

one. It was prepared by as many as six different people at six different times: people who never met together as a team or discussed how the assets they advised you on should be titled to achieve your estate plan. The following plans may be applicable to your current situation:

It would be unusual if the person who prepared your deed asked you how you would like to have it titled.

THE DEED TO YOUR HOME OR OTHER PROPERTY

If you are married, when the title agent or attorney prepared the deed for your home, he probably designated the deed as tenants by the entireties *without asking you.* In addition, if you have other jointly owned assets, it would be unusual for you to have been asked how you would like to have them titled when the deeds were prepared.

LIFE INSURANCE

When you purchased your life insurance, the agent asked you to name the beneficiary of the policy. That beneficiary designation is a part of your estate plan.

IRAS

When you first invested in an IRA at the bank or through a mutual fund, you named a beneficiary. Determining who the recipient of that IRA will be at your death is part of your estate plan.

ANNUITIES

Annuity contracts name a designated beneficiary to receive the annuity funds at the death of the owner. The investment advisor asked you, at some point, who should be named as the beneficiary of your annuities.

TRANSFER ON DEATH ACCOUNTS

Any securities that you registered with your investment advisor as a T.O.D. account is a part of your estate plan.

YOUR WILL

Lastly, there is your will, the one plan that probably received the most thoughtful consideration. The person who prepared your will, however, may not have confirmed how your name is listed on your deed or who the beneficiaries are of your life insurance, IRAs, annuities, and transfer on death accounts. As you can see, it is critical to approach estate planning from a *comprehensive* perspective, one that considers all angles and involves all the members of your team working together.

Post-Mortem Estate Planning

One interesting aspect of estate planning is called post-mortem estate planning. This refers to strategies to complete or make corrections to an estate plan after one's death. There are a number of tax elections that can be done post-mortem as well as the right of the surviving spouse to elect against the will. Another area of post-mortem estate planning relates to the use of DISCLAIMERS. In the sections that follow, we will briefly discuss the spousal election rights and the disclaimers as used in post-mortem estate planning.

Surviving Spouse's Right to Elect Against the Will

When a married person in Pennsylvania dies, no matter what their will, living trust or estate plan specifies, their surviving spouse has a *legal right* to take one-third of the augmented estate of the deceased spouse. This is known as the ELECTIVE SHARE rule. (The term augmented estate refers to the estate of the deceased spouse with adjustments made for certain distributions made during lifetime.) The public policy behind the Pennsylvania elective share rule is to prevent one spouse from disinheriting the other by confirming that the surviving spouse will at least have a *minimal* share of the decedent's estate.

> The elective share rule is an election that the surviving spouse must affirmatively make in order to receive the one-third share. The request for election must be filed no later than six months after the death of the spouse.

The assets over which the surviving spouse has the right to make the election include that which passes from the deceased spouse by will or intestacy. In addition, assets conveyed by the decedent during marriage to himself or herself and another with rights of survivorships are also included in the augmented estate. Lastly, assets that were given away by the decedent within one year of death to the extent that the gift exceeded $3,000.00 to each donee and certain annuities are subject to this election. (Life insurance is not included in the estate for purposes of calculating the one-third amount.)

This is a legal right that can be lost if one spouse forfeits their right by deserting the deceased spouse during their lifetime. Also, the use of a PREMARITAL AGREEMENT may eliminate the possibility of a spouse electing against the will.

DISCLAIMERS

One can disclaim an interest in an asset that they are entitled to receive as an inheritance under a will. One can also disclaim or refuse to accept an interest that they are entitled to receive under the beneficiary designation of life insurance or an IRA. Lastly, one could disclaim an interest that they would receive by being a joint owner of an asset if one of the other joint owners should die. Pennsylvania law states that a person "to whom an interest in property would have evolved by whatever means" has a right to disclaim that interest. This means that you can disclaim any interest in any asset that you are entitled to receive and give up any rights that you would have in that interest. The interest disclaimed can be either the entire interest or a portion of the interest.

Disclaimer is a legal term that refers to the refusal to accept an interest in an asset.

The requirements for a valid disclaimer are: (1) it must describe the interest disclaimed, (2) it must declare that the disclaimant is in fact disclaiming the interest, and (3) it must be signed by the disclaimant.

The disclaimer is *irrevocable* and the assets cannot be retrieved once it has been disclaimed. In the event of a disclaimer, the law treats the disclaimant as having predeceased the decedent and the interest will pass as though the disclaimant had died before the transfer was made. For this reason, one should be diligent in confirming exactly to whom the disclaimed interest will go once the disclaimer is filed.

Why Would Someone Choose To Disclaim?

Disclaiming is often done for federal tax purposes. The disclaimer must qualify under the Internal Revenue Code §2518 as well as Pennsylvania law when disclaiming for federal tax purposes. The requirements under Internal Revenue Code §2518 for a qualified disclaimer are as follows:

- The disclaimer must be an irrevocable refusal to accept an interest;
- The disclaimer must be in writing;
- The disclaimer must be delivered to the transferor or the holder of the legal title to the assets to which the interest relates no later than nine months after the date of the transfer creating the interest or the date disclaimant becomes twenty-one;
- The disclaimant must not have accepted the disclaimed interest or any of its benefits; and
- The disclaimed interest must pass without any direction on the part of the disclaimant.

One key provision regarding disclaimers is that they must be filed before accepting any interest in the assets being disclaimed. Once one has accepted the benefit of any assets, he or she will be barred from disclaiming any interest in the assets accepted.

WHAT ARE THE BENEFITS OF DISCLAIMING?

As a part of post-mortem estate planning, disclaiming is a strategy often used to do federal estate tax planning after death. For example, if husband had CREDIT SHELTER TRUST provisions in his will (*which are discussed in detail in Chapter 9*) but owned all of his assets jointly with his wife, the only way that assets could be used to fund husband's credit shelter trust after his death would be for his wife to disclaim her husband's one-half interest in the joint assets that she would inherit by operation of law. As a result of her disclaimer, the husband's one-half interest does not go to the wife by operation of law; instead, the husband's interest is now controlled by his will and will be available to fund his credit shelter trust.

The use of a disclaimer will permit assets to pass to others at lower tax rates.

Another use of disclaimers is with annuities. For example, Mrs. Jones owns a $100,000.00 annuity that is payable to the children of her first marriage at her death. Upon her death, it is determined that there would be state inheritance tax and federal estate tax upon the amounts inherited by her children. If, in this case, the children were to disclaim their interests in the annuity, the annuity would be payable to Mrs. Smith's estate. Estate assets are controlled by her will, and Mrs. Smith's will directs that her assets be given to her husband to qualify for the marital deduction. The result of her children's disclaimer is that no tax is due on the annuities. There are many other instances where the use of a disclaimer will permit assets to pass to others at lower tax rates.

How Are Disclaimers Invoked?

Once it is determined that the estate plan of a deceased person would be improved if one of the beneficiaries disclaimed their interest, notice of their intent to disclaim must be provided to the transferor of the interest no later than *nine months after the date of death.* That notice must be given directly to the transferor. A copy of the notice can be filed at the county register of wills office and date-stamped to confirm the timing of the disclaimer.

Disclaimer of Jointly Owned Assets

The IRS permits jointly owned assets to be disclaimed whether the jointly owned assets are held as joint tenants with rights of survivorship or held by husband and wife as tenants by the entireties. In either case, the surviving joint tenant is permitted to file a disclaimer within *nine months* of the date of death of the first joint tenant to die disclaiming the asset interest they are entitled to receive by operation of law.

Rules Regarding Disclaimers by a Surviving Spouse of Jointly Owned Assets in Pennsylvania

All jointly owned assets can be placed in one of two categories.

Category #1

Depending on who contributed the funds into the account, it may be possible for a surviving spouse to disclaim the entire balance in such an account within nine months of the first spouse's death. This includes joint accounts created in banks, brokerage firms and other investment accounts such as mutual funds.

Category #2

The second category includes joint tenancies created in all other types of assets. If the assets in this category were owned solely by the two spouses, it is only possible for a surviving spouse to disclaim a maximum of one-half of the interest in their joint assets when the first spouse dies.

Summary

Before you can define what estate planning is, you must recognize the many assets that make up your estate. Once those assets are listed, you can identify if they are probate or non-probate assets and then determine if you have the proper beneficiaries designated and a clear understanding of what is and is not governed by your will. As life situations change and as you may have had the input of several different professionals at different times, it's important to ensure that your plan is up to date, comprehensive, and consistent with your goals.

Where joint ownership is concerned, you can confirm that your wishes are carried out by having a clear understanding of the three types of joint ownership recognized by the State of Pennsylvania. Also, it is important to understand the benefits of elective share rule and post-mortem estate planning such as disclaimers.

Part II

Who Will Manage Your Affairs If You Become Incapacitated?

"Dig a well before you are thirsty."

– Chinese proverb

3

Planning for Incapacity

Topics Include

Management by Court-Appointed Guardian
Management by Power of Attorney
Management by Trustee
Healthcare Power of Attorney
The Living Will
Paying for Long-Term Care
Planning for Nursing Home Costs
Long-Term Care Insurance
Trusts for Family Members with Disabilities

Introduction

In his book, *Cyclops Awakes: A Newspaperman Fights Back after a Massive Stroke,* former UPI correspondent John Mantle describes life before and after suffering a stroke. Before: piloting small planes, running a newspaper with his wife, enjoying his Gold Wing motorcycle and the outdoors of North and South

Carolina. Afterward: loss of mobility, loss of clarity in speech, loss of income and adjusting to dependency while reaching for rehabilitation. Fortunately, Mantle did make an astounding recovery, and, also fortunately, he had the foresight to purchase disability insurance.

Everyone, especially as they approach mid-life or when they suddenly realize they qualify for a senior citizen discount, wonders what will happen to them if they become incapacitated, either short term or long term. A heart attack, a stroke, a battle with cancer, or simply slipping on an icy sidewalk can change our life in ways we really don't like to think about. How will the medical bills be paid? Who will help with preparing meals or driving me to doctor appointments? Will I have to move in with my children? What if I have no children or what if they live far away and cannot help? What if I'm already caring for an ill spouse or elderly parent...*I can't afford to get sick!*

Failure to make any plans to deal with incapacity could result in a court-appointed guardian managing your affairs.

While the natural tendency is to avoid topics that make us uncomfortable, consciously considering worst case scenarios and doing whatever possible now, while in good health, to prepare as best one can is reassuring. In this chapter, I will describe planning strategies to address the concerns that arise in the event you do become incapacitated. This chapter also covers helpful plans in case of the INCAPACITY of a family member, whether a child (adult or minor) that is disabled or one of your parents who is in a nursing home or has other needs. Planning for possible incapacity involves maintaining the financial well being of the incapacitated person as well as planning for his or her personal care. Failure to make any plans to deal with incapacity could result in a court-appointed GUARDIAN managing your affairs. Few people would want a complete stranger to handle their affairs. Guardianship can be avoided through careful planning.

Who Will Manage Your Assets If You Become Incapacitated?

If you were determined to be incapacitated, and did not make any plans, you may require a court-appointed guardian. Pennsylvania law defines an incapacitated person as "an adult whose ability to receive and evaluate information effectively and communicate decisions in any way is impaired to such a significant extent that he is partially or totally unable to manage his financial resources or to meet essential requirements for his physical health and safety." The mere presence of mental illness or a physical disability does not render one an incapacitated person. People who are disabled do not lose their right to self-determination simply because they are disabled.

Management by Your Court-Appointed Guardian

Two forms of guardianship can be enacted: plenary guardianship and limited guardianship.

If no one has previously been designated by the incapacitated person to act as guardian, the court may do so. If the court finds that a person is incapacitated and in need of guardianship services, two forms of guardianship can be enacted: plenary guardianship and limited guardianship. In plenary guardianship, full and *total legal responsibility* is given to the court-appointed guardian. In limited guardianships, the guardian's authority is *limited* in some way by the court decree appointing the guardian. For example, the guardianship can be limited to only managing the person's finances, or it could be limited to a certain period of time.

The expense, publicity and delay caused by the hearings, court deliberations and issuance of a court order can all be avoided by proper planning.

Power of Attorney & Management by Your Named Agent

As I mentioned earlier, few people would choose to have a stranger make all their financial and healthcare decisions for them. All the more reason why it is so important to have plans in place in the event you become incapacitated. Let's look at the documents that can be prepared before illness or injury strike.

A POWER OF ATTORNEY is a document that gives another person or institution named by you the right to take certain actions on your behalf. The scope of actions authorized are written within the power of attorney. You are the PRINCIPAL who signs the power of attorney and the

Plenary Guardianship

Total responsibility for the incapacitated person. Responsibility over health care, finances, assets, living arrangements, property … total responsibility.

Limited Guardianships

Responsibility is specified by court decree. For example: managing finances, making healthcare decisions, handling living arrangements, etc.

How Guardianship Is Established by the Court

1. Petition is filed with the court.
2. Notice is given to the alleged incapacitated person and their next of kin.
3. A time and place (in the county where the person lives) of a court hearing to determine incapacity is set.
4. Evidence is presented regarding the person's incapacity.
5. The court determines if there is a need for guardianship.
6. The court appoints: an individual, a corporate fiduciary, or a county agency as guardian.
7. The guardian is required to file an annual report and accounting with the court.

person given the authority to act on your behalf is called the AGENT. A valid power of attorney that names an appropriate agent avoids the guardianship procedure, provided there are no guardianship services needed that are not specified in the power of attorney.

For powers of attorney signed after April 12, 2000, there are two new requirements. First, the first page of a power of attorney must have a notice in capital letters signed by the principal. The second change is that the power of attorney must have an acknowledgment affixed to it signed by the agent. (*See form on page 44.*)

With regard to the power of attorney, it is important to understand that the death of the principal ends the authority of the agent.

> A power of attorney can be "durable," which means it remains in effect even if you become incapacitated. After 1992, all powers of attorney signed in Pennsylvania are presumed to be durable unless specifically designated otherwise. Since there is no reason not to use the word "durable," it is preferred that the word be used, if your intent is that your agent would continue to have legal authority as agent even if you become incapacitated.

The death of the principal ends the authority of the agent.

In other words, when you die, your agent no longer has any authority to act on your behalf. Sometimes children who have served as agent under a power of attorney for an elderly parent attempt to withdraw money from the bank to pay funeral expenses after their parent has died. They are surprised to discover that the bank no longer honors the power of attorney, because the parent is deceased. Only the executor named in the will can gain access to the money after the death of a parent.

A power of attorney can be effective immediately or it can give the agent the authority to act only after the principal becomes incapacitated. The latter is known as a SPRINGING POWER OF ATTORNEY. One difficulty with the springing power of attorney is that in order to gain the legal authority to serve as the agent, the agent must have proof that the principal is incapacitated. This proof can generally be provided by a certification of incapacity by a physician, but some banks or investment firms might prefer a court order of incapacity. This defeats the reason for having a power of attorney. Yet, even though court proceedings may be necessary, at least the person named as agent could take control rather than a stranger appointed by the court.

It should be noted that if a power of attorney is immediately effective, it should not be used by the agent, if the principal is capable of making decisions on his or her own behalf (unless directed to do so by the principal).

Husbands and wives usually appoint each other as their agents, and name adult children as successor agents. If husband and wife each

Notice

THE PURPOSE OF THIS POWER OF ATTORNEY IS TO GIVE THE PERSON YOU DESIGNATE (YOUR "AGENT") BROAD POWERS TO HANDLE YOUR ASSETS, WHICH MAY INCLUDE POWERS TO SELL OR OTHERWISE DISPOSE OF ANY REAL OR PERSONAL PROPERTY WITHOUT ADVANCE NOTICE TO YOU OR APPROVAL BY YOU.

THIS POWER OF ATTORNEY DOES NOT IMPOSE A DUTY ON YOUR AGENT TO EXERCISE GRANTED POWERS, BUT WHEN POWERS ARE EXERCISED, YOUR AGENT MUST USE DUE CARE TO ACT FOR YOUR BENEFIT AND IN ACCORDANCE WITH THIS POWER OF ATTORNEY.

YOUR AGENT MAY EXERCISE THE POWERS GIVEN HERE THROUGHOUT YOUR LIFETIME, EVEN AFTER YOU BECOME INCAPACITATED, UNLESS YOU EXPRESSLY LIMIT THE DURATION OF THESE POWERS OR YOU REVOKE THESE POWERS OR A COURT ACTING ON YOUR BEHALF TERMINATES YOUR AGENT'S AUTHORITY

YOUR AGENT MUST KEEP YOUR FUNDS SEPARATE FROM YOUR AGENT'S FUNDS.

A COURT CAN TAKE AWAY THE POWERS OF YOUR AGENT IF IT FINDS YOUR AGENT IS NOT ACTING PROPERLY.

THE POWERS AND DUTIES OF AN AGENT UNDER A POWER OF ATTORNEY ARE EXPLAINED MORE FULLY IN 20 PA.C.S. CH. 56.

IF THERE IS ANYTHING ABOUT THIS FORM THAT YOU DO NOT UNDERSTAND, YOU SHOULD ASK A LAWYER OF YOUR OWN CHOOSING TO EXPLAIN IT TO YOU.

I HAVE READ OR HAD EXPLAINED TO ME THIS NOTICE AND I UNDERSTAND ITS CONTENTS.

____________________________ __________
(PRINCIPAL) (DATE)

Agent Acknowledgement

I, ____________________________, have read the attached power of attorney and am the person identified as the agent for the principal. I hereby acknowledge that in the absence of a specific provision to the contrary in the power of attorney or in 20 PA.C.S., Chapter 56 when I act as agent:

I shall exercise the powers for the benefit of the principal.

I shall keep the assets of the principal separate from my assets.

I shall exercise reasonable caution and prudence.

I shall keep a full and accurate record of all actions, receipts and disbursements on behalf of the principal.

____________________________ __________
(AGENT) (DATE)

name the other as the initial agent, there is little danger in having an immediate power of attorney. Indeed, having an immediate power of attorney would be a help if one spouse is unavailable to sign any documents that would require both signatures, such as a deed for the sale of real estate.

There is no restriction as to the number of people that can be named as agent in a power of attorney. The law provides a list of specified powers that may be incorporated into your power of attorney. These powers are not required to be listed in full, but can be referred to in summary form. Listing in full, however, will confirm to others your intent. You may also grant powers to your agents that are in addition to those listed in the law.

Mr. and Mrs. Miller & Their Not-So-Secret Agents

Mr. and Mrs. Miller have three children. They can appoint each other as primary agent and their three children as alternate agents with the provision that any one of the three children can act alone as agent under the power of attorney. An alternative is to require the signatures of all three children to take any action using the power of attorney, or, that child A would serve, but if unavailable then child B would serve as alternate, and child C as successor alternate.

MANAGEMENT BY THE SUCCESSOR TRUSTEE NAMED IN YOUR LIVING TRUST

LIVING TRUSTS are another strategy to plan for incapacity. In a living trust you can appoint a primary trustee and a successor trustee (who would control the assets should the primary trustee become incapacitated). (*For more information on living trusts, see Chapter 5.*)

Essential Benefits of Power of Attorney

1. It provides a means to manage the finances of the incapacitated person. There is no need to tie up investments during the course of a guardianship procedure.
2. It can give permission to the agent to make gifts on behalf of the principal. In order for an incapacitated person's agent to make gifts, he or she must have that authority specified in the power of attorney.
3. If husband and wife owned real estate jointly, in order to sell the real estate, both signatures would be required. If one spouse is incapacitated, a guardianship hearing could be avoided with a power of attorney.

Who Will Make Your Healthcare Decisions If You Become Incapacitated?

HEALTHCARE POWER OF ATTORNEY

Pennsylvania's power of attorney law is limited regarding health-care decisions. Current law states only that you (the principal) may grant your agent the power to authorize your admission to a medical, nursing, residential, or similar facility, and enter into agreements for your care, and also to authorize medical and surgical procedures. Many other states have laws that define what are known as HEALTHCARE POWERS OF ATTORNEY. These are powers of attorney used to appoint a health-care agent to make healthcare decisions for the principal including decisions relating to life sustaining treatment.

THE LIVING WILL (ADVANCE MEDICAL DIRECTIVE)

Those who are in their fifties and sixties today will most likely live longer lives than their parents or grandparents did. Advances in the field of medical care and lifestyle differences make it possible for

> Although Pennsylvania law does not specifically provide for a healthcare power of attorney, many attorneys have prepared such documents for their clients, and a recent court case has confirmed the authority of a healthcare agent named in a healthcare power of attorney to act on behalf of the principal. The language in a healthcare power of attorney should be very specific as to your intent, to assist your agent with understanding exactly what you want. The healthcare power of attorney can include all of the same language that appears in the living will discussed in the next section of this book. A healthcare power of attorney usually does not become legally binding unless the principal is unable to make his or her wishes known.

many people to live fully and vibrantly well into their eighties. Adults of all ages have definite beliefs and desires concerning their wishes should they become incapacitated and dependent on medical technology to keep them alive. Without a living will, however, someone else will be responsible for making decisions regarding your end-of-life care.

A LIVING WILL is a document that gives directions to your treating physicians concerning end-of-life care in the event you become unable to communicate due to permanent unconsciousness or terminal illness and incapacity. The document can take any form, but it must be signed and witnessed by two others. *(See a sample living will in Appendix 2 of this book.)*

Pennsylvania citizens eighteen years or older have a right to declare their desires regarding medical treatment.

The living will is activated only under the following circumstances:

1. You must be incapacitated and *either*
2. permanently unconscious (in a coma from which you are never expected to awaken), or
3. terminally ill.

Two physicians must certify in writing that you meet the conditions of *either* (2) or (3). Also, a copy of the living will must be given to the treating physician.

Pennsylvania citizens eighteen years or older (or who have graduated from high school) have a right to declare their desires regarding medical treatment to be initiated, continued, withheld or withdrawn. Living wills in Pennsylvania also include the opportunity to designate another person to make treatment decisions as a surrogate decision maker. The role of the surrogate is to make medical treatment decisions on your behalf.

Who Will Pay for Your Care If You Cannot Take Care of Yourself?

PAYING FOR LONG-TERM CARE AT HOME OR IN A LONG-TERM CARE FACILITY

Life expectancy has increased with each generation, yet so have healthcare costs. A growing concern of many Pennsylvanians is depleting their assets to pay for nursing home care. The average monthly cost of nursing home care in Pennsylvania is $5,250.83 (as of 2001). The average annual cost of long-term care: $63,000+. A three-year stay in a nursing home: $189,000. Two questions immediately arise: "Who will pay for these services?" and "Will I outlive my money by paying for these services?"

Medical assistance is the only government benefit available to provide money for long-term nursing home care.

Many people assume that the government will pay for their nursing home care, but there is no government program established to pay the nursing home or long-term care expenses of Pennsylvanians who can afford to pay for these services themselves.

The government has established two insurance programs that *may* pay for these healthcare services: Medicare and MEDICAID. Medicare is a government health insurance program with an automatic enrollment for all persons regardless of income who are age sixty-five or older and eligible for social security retirement benefits. The coverage offered by Medicare is for skilled nursing home care for a *maximum of twenty days* when nursing home residency immediately follows qualified hospitalization. Not every hospital patient qualifies for this coverage. For days twenty-one through one hundred Medicare *pays only a portion* of

> Based on data compiled by the Center for Applied Research and Policy Analysis in a report titled "Long-Term Care 2000: Statistics and Information," the following is the breakdown of who pays for long-term care in Pennsylvania:
>
> - Medical assistance (Medicaid) 63%
> - Private pay 23%
> - Medicare 10%
> - Veteran's Administration 2%
> - Private long-term-care insurance 2%

expenses. After one hundred days in a nursing home, Medicare pays *nothing.* Clearly, Medicare is not a readily available source of funds to pay for your long-term care.

Medicaid, or MEDICAL ASSISTANCE as it is known in Pennsylvania, is the only government benefit available to provide money for long-term nursing home care. Medicaid is a joint federal-state program providing medical assistance for persons with very few assets who are aged, blind or disabled. Each state administers its federal Medicaid program according to general standards set by Congress. In Pennsylvania, the department of public welfare oversees Medicaid. In order to determine the eligibility of an applicant to receive Medicaid payments for nursing home care, the department of public welfare will consider the applicant's income and resources as well as that of the applicant's spouse to determine whether or not the applicant qualifies for medical assistance based on financial need.

Medical Assistance Planning for Nursing Home Costs

MEDICAL ASSISTANCE

Medical assistance is a welfare program intended for those who cannot afford medical and/or nursing home care. Because of the increasing cost of such care, many people are interested in arranging their income and assets so that they can qualify for medical assistance while at the same time keeping their assets for their family.

WHO CAN QUALIFY FOR MEDICAL ASSISTANCE?

Many people are interested in arranging their income and assets so that they can qualify for medical assistance.

In order to qualify for medical assistance, you must meet certain requirements based upon financial need, medical need and state residency. There are two financial prerequisites necessary in order to qualify for medical assistance in Pennsylvania: the assets test and the income test.

The Assets Test

When an application is made to the department of public welfare for medical assistance, the assets of the applicant are reviewed. All assets of the applicant are divided into one of the two following categories:

- **Available Resources:** This term refers to the applicant's resources available to pay for the cost of care. Everything owned by the applicant is considered an available resource except for those specifically exempted by law.
- **Unavailable Resources:** Resources that the applicant (and the applicant's spouse if married) is permitted to own and still qualify for medical assistance. (The applicant's spouse is known as the "community spouse.")

What is the maximum total allowable available resources an applicant can have and still qualify for medical assistance? $2,400 (at the time of publication). If an applicant has more than $2,400 in available resources, the applicant does not qualify for medical assistance.

A portion of the total resources owned by both the spouse living in a nursing home and the spouse living in the community is legally protected for the use of the community spouse. This is the portion that is called the "protected spousal share," and it is not considered an available resource to pay for nursing home care. The protected spousal share that the community spouse is entitled to keep is equal to one half of the value of the total combined resources of the applicant and the community spouse up to a maximum of $87,000 (with the minimum of

Assets You May Keep & Still Qualify for Medical Assitance

In considering an applicant's assets, unavailable resources are

- applicant's personal residence,
- household goods,
- one motor vehicle,
- burial plot and irrevocable burial reserve in a reasonable amount,
- life insurance (whole life with cash value up to a maximum of $1,000 and term policies to any value), and
- assets used in a trade or business essential to self support.
- The following assets are also exempt if the applicant is married: community spouse's IRA, 401(k), pension funds, Keogh plan, community spouse's "protected spousal share."

$17,400). This amount is in addition to the $2,400 of available assets allowed to the nursing home spouse. Once the community spouse is institutionalized, the resources of each are counted separately. These dollar amounts change every year.

The Income Test

All income of the applicant, except for a $30 per month allowance for personal needs, is considered available to pay for healthcare. This includes income from social security and private pensions as well as any other income including interest and dividends from investments.

The Hurly Appeal

The MMMNA is the minimum amount needed to maintain the community spouse at home.

The community spouse is permitted to have a minimum monthly maintenance needs allowance (also known as MMMNA). The MMMNA is the minimum amount needed to maintain the community spouse at home. This amount changes every year. As of July 1, 2001, it was $1,452 of income per month. In situations where the amount of income earned by the community spouse is *below* the MMMNA amount, the community spouse may elect to receive income from the institutionalized spouse to increase the monthly income of the community spouse to the minimum monthly allowance.

Community spouses with income below the MMMNA amount also have a strategy to increase their income known as a HURLY APPEAL, so named because of a court case. In the Hurley case, it was determined that the value of the protected spousal share could be increased to the amount necessary to produce enough income to equal the MMMNA. The additional amount of the protected spousal share is determined by calculating the value of a commercial annuity that would generate the income necessary to equal the MMMNA amount. The community spouse is not required to purchase a commercial annuity but is deemed to have the income that would be derived if such an annuity were purchased.

The Transfer of Assets Rule

Giving away assets before entering a long-term care facility can reduce your options.

Since medical assistance payments are based on need, most of those who do not qualify fail to qualify because they have too many assets. Therefore, many believe that they will qualify for medical assistance by simply giving away all of their assets and impoverishing themselves. The practice of giving away assets to qualify for government benefits has caused much discussion concerning the moral and ethical issues it raises. In addition, giving away assets before entering a long-term care facility can reduce your options regarding the type of facility that you enter. Many retirement communities do not depend on government programs, and only those residents who can pay for their services are admitted.

To discourage such gift giving, the department of public welfare requires that any assets given away during a look-back period must be included as an available resource to the applicant. If gifts were given during this period of time, medical assistance will be denied for a specified period of time.

The Look-Back Period

The look-back period begins on the day that the applicant is both institutionalized and applies for medical assistance. When one applies for medical assistance, the department of public welfare looks back three years from the date of application to determine if gifts were made to individuals and five years to see if any gifts were made to or from trusts. If any gifts were made, the applicant will be ineligible to receive medical assistance for a specified period of time.

If gifts were made during the look-back period, the period of time that the applicant is denied medical assistance is equal to the number of months of nursing home care the applicant could have paid for using the money that was given away. To calculate this period of time, the department of public welfare will divide the total value of gifts given by the average monthly rate for nursing home care. The period of ineligibility begins upon the date of transfer.

> If Mother transferred $100,000 to her children thirty days before she entered a nursing home and applied for medical assistance, she would be denied medical assistance benefits for a period of time equal to $100,000 (the amount of the gift) divided by $5,250.83 (the average monthly rate) which equals nineteen months of ineligibility for medical assistance.

Permitted Transfers

Some transfers during the look-back period are permitted. Permitted transfers include any transfer to a spouse or, under limited exceptions, transfers of a residence. If either spouse makes a gift, both can be denied benefits for up to thirty-six months regardless of which one enters a nursing home.

One should always retain enough assets to pay for care during any period of ineligibility.

Transfer Risks

Transferring assets in order to qualify for medical assistance carries with it certain risks. The risks involving transfers are based on the fact that transferred assets are irrevocably owned by the transferee who may squander the assets or lose them in a divorce or bankruptcy. In addition, there are numerous tax traps that must be considered. Clearly, one should retain enough assets to pay for care during any period of ineligibility. Transfers of assets should not be undertaken without accurate professional legal advice from an attorney who regularly practices in this area of law.

TRANSFER STRATEGIES

A number of transfer strategies have developed to assist one in qualifying for medical assistance while maximizing the amount of assets passed on to family and heirs. It cannot be overstated that the permissibility of these strategies is subject to change at a moment's notice. This is an *ever-changing* area of law, and a strategy that is acceptable today may be no longer permitted tomorrow. It is important to consult with experienced legal counsel before engaging in any of these strategies.

MEDICAL ASSISTANCE ESTATE RECOVERY PROGRAM

An experienced elder law attorney can help create the best plan for your situation by choosing the best techniques available at the time you are making your plans.

The department of public welfare is charged with recovering from the probate estate of individuals aged fifty-five and over any amounts paid on behalf of the decedent by the state for medical assistance during the last five years of his life. The executor is required to send notice to the department of public welfare to ask if a claim exists. If the decedent is survived by a spouse living in the house, the department must postpone collection until after his or her death. It is interesting to note that assets held in a REVOCABLE LIVING TRUST are not probate estate assets and are not currently subject to this program. The department of public welfare, however, holds that transfer of a principal residence of applicant or applicant's spouse into a revocable living trust causes it to lose its status as an unavailable resource. In addition, one cannot qualify for medical assistance until assets held in such a trust meet the financial requirement for eligibility, meaning that they cannot exceed $2,400.

THE USE OF TRUSTS IN MEDICAL ASSISTANCE PLANNING

There are no benefits using revocable living trusts when it comes to medical assistance planning in Pennsylvania. There are a few IRREVOCABLE TRUSTS that can be utilized to protect assets from long-term care costs. Transfer to trusts incur the five year look-back penalty or must be TESTAMENTARY. Nevertheless, in the right circumstances, irrevocable trusts can be excellent planning tools.

HOW TO APPLY FOR MEDICAL ASSISTANCE (MEDICAID)

The process for applying for medical assistance has two aspects:

1. **Medical qualification.** The office of the aging in your county will assist with the medical evaluation required for medical assistance.
2. **Financial need.** The determination of financial need is administered locally through your county assistance office. A form known as the "Department of Public Welfare Admissions Notice Packet" contains in it the information and paperwork necessary to permit the county assistance office to perform a resource assessment and determine the financial needs for medical assistance.

> You should get expert advice as soon as the need for long-term care becomes evident. To delay seeking advice from a qualified professional advisor may result in lost benefits.

Long-Term Care Insurance

Long-term care is care that is needed for long periods of time and is not considered to be rehabilitative.

Many people consider long-term care to be only care that is given to senior citizens and the elderly in skilled-care nursing homes. Long-term care, however, includes a broad spectrum of care. Long-term care could refer to a person residing in a skilled nursing facility receiving twenty-four hour care under the supervision of a physician. On the other hand, it could refer to a person only receiving custodial care, (help with bathing, dressing and eating). Long-term care is care that is needed for long periods of time and is not considered to be rehabilitative. Long-term care can be provided in a nursing home setting, in the recipient's own home, or in a group setting such as an assisted living facility.

WHO SHOULD CONSIDER LONG-TERM CARE INSURANCE?

For many, the prospects of qualifying for medical assistance are not encouraging, so a growing number of people are purchasing long-term care insurance. You must take into account your age and the size of your estate to determine whether this type of insurance is for you.

Age

According to experts in the field, long-term care insurance can be most beneficial to those between the ages of fifty-five and seventy-five. Many in this age group, however, are focused on accumulating assets for future retirement and are reluctant to spend the money for a future need they feel they may never have. Nevertheless, this is an ideal age to acquire the coverage because of the lower rates.

Estate Size

Those with estates of between $150,000 and $2 million are good candidates to consider long-term care insurance. People with estates this size can usually afford to pay the premium. A typical individual with an estate size in this range is planning to use his assets to live on during his retirement years and still have something left over to pass on to his heirs. Those with estates over $2 million may not need long-term care insurance, because they would have the income necessary to pay for long-term care if needed. Those with less than $150,000 may find the premiums to be too high relative to the size of their estate.

> For planning purposes, one should presume that it would take a $1 million diversified investment portfolio to produce sufficient income to pay the annual costs of nursing home or home care.

THE PURPOSE OF LONG-TERM CARE INSURANCE

Insurance coverage might be necessary if an estate is "illiquid." In other words it does not have the cash to pay for nursing home care.

Long-term care insurance should also be considered by those desiring to maintain their independence.

Insurance proceeds would also be helpful to pay for nursing home care during the look-back period of thirty-six months (if gifts are made at the time of entering a nursing home). Some people purchase long-term care insurance to pay for only the look-back period, because after that they will qualify for medical assistance.

Long-term care insurance should also be considered by those desiring to maintain their independence, because it can provide them with the money needed for them to stay at home. In addition, long-term care insurance benefits would permit you to avoid depending upon your children for care and would eliminate financial concerns of a long lifetime. Long-term care insurance would also permit retaining some inheritance for one's children.

WHAT TO LOOK FOR IN LONG-TERM CARE COVERAGE

Levels of Care Covered

The levels of care paid for by the various long-term care insurance companies include nursing home coverage for skilled, intermediate, and custodial care. In addition to paying for nursing home expenses, many policies now also provide for home care coverage. Home care coverage should be investigated closely in the contract. If available, it can provide such services as skilled care, adult day-care, home health aides and personal care attendants, all while you stay in your home. Coverage for assisted living care, respite care and inflation protection should also be considered when shopping for long-term care insurance.

Length of Time of Coverage

As for the benefit period, insurance companies typically offer a choice of benefit periods between two years and six years or even lifetime benefits. The longer the benefit period, of course, the more expensive the policy. Considering the expense of coverage, typical guidelines are that if you are under sixty years of age, lifetime coverage would be preferred. For those who are over eighty years of age, many commentators suggest three to five years of coverage. For those between sixty and eighty years of age, perhaps a minimum term of three years with the length of the term dictated by cash resources. The probability of staying in a nursing home more than five years is so low that some recommend buying coverage for a four or five year period as opposed to lifetime. These guidelines are only intended to give you an idea of some long-term care insurance strategies. Before purchasing long-term care insurance it is important to work with a professional advisor experienced in this area.

> The costs of long-term care, whether in a nursing home or at your home, are expected to continue to rise significantly. A comprehensive approach to estate planning requires serious consideration of long-term care insurance. The options are so wide ranging that you should be able to custom fit coverage to your specific needs and desires. Married couples should invest in coverage for both spouses.

THE BASIC ELEMENTS OF A LONG-TERM CARE INSURANCE CONTRACT

Daily Benefit

This is the amount of money that the policy will pay for each day. The average daily cost of skilled care in the area in which you wish to live in retirement should be used to determine an adequate DAILY BENEFIT.

Elimination Period

This is the period of time that one must go without benefits after the commencement of the event that triggers the claim. Benefits will begin to be paid to the insured only after this period of time. There are no benefits paid during the elimination period. Elimination periods can run from zero to as long as one year. The most common periods, however, are generally from twenty to sixty days.

Benefit Period

This is the period of time during which benefits will be paid at the full daily rate. Typical periods are two, three, four, five, six years or lifetime. When considering the BENEFIT PERIOD of policies, it is important to consider both long-term care and short-term care. Medicare strictly limits the number of days of coverage for hospitalization and skilled nursing services. The result is that more people are being required to pay for REHABILITATIVE CARE (SHORT-TERM CARE). Long-term care policies that have a RESTORATION OF BENEFITS clause would cover these short-term rehabilitative periods based on such events as stroke or hip fracture.

Trusts for Family Members with Disabilities

Many parents do not know who will care for their disabled child after they are gone.

One of the more serious concerns facing the parents of a disabled child is knowing who will care for their child after the parents die or become incapacitated. A significant number of families face this unique challenge. A study by the University of Illinois at Chicago revealed that nearly 500,000 disabled adults live with at least one parent who is at least sixty years old. Unfortunately, many of those parents do not know who will care for their disabled child after they are gone. Providing financial stability for such children is fairly easy for parents who have the resources, but providing *personal* care for such children may be a challenge. Parents whose resources may already be depleted after many years of caring for their child face both the financial and the practical issues. In some cases siblings will step in to continue to care for the disabled, but often it is the state that will take care of them.

WHAT ARE SPECIAL NEEDS TRUSTS & SUPPLEMENTAL NEEDS TRUSTS?

Experts predict that one of the most significant growth areas of elder law in the coming years will deal with two types of trusts, the special needs trust and the supplemental needs trust. Before a discussion of these trusts can be undertaken, it is important to comment upon the confusing language surrounding these trusts. Despite their similar names, experts generally differentiate between a supplemental needs trust and a special needs trust.

Special needs trusts are created by a family member or other person on behalf of a disabled beneficiary using the beneficiary's own funds. In order to continue the beneficiary's eligibility for government benefits, a special needs trust must provide that upon the death of the disabled beneficiary, the trust must reimburse the state for any Medicaid benefits it has paid to the disabled beneficiary before any other beneficiaries can receive any distribution. Based on the federal law that permits such trusts, they are also known as (d)(4)(A) trusts.

The supplemental needs trust is established to protect the beneficiary's eligibility to receive government benefits.

The supplemental needs trust, like the special needs trust, is established to protect the beneficiary's eligibility to receive government benefits. Supplemental needs trusts, however, are generally established by people who are not concerned about qualifying for government benefits themselves, and who use their own money to fund the trust. Since the person establishing the supplemental needs trust has no need for government benefits, a supplemental needs trust is permitted to distribute the remainder of the trust to beneficiaries after the death of the disabled beneficiary, without regard for reimbursement to the state for any Medicaid payments received by the disabled beneficiary.

When a special needs trust is established for a disabled individual using the disabled individual's own funds, it is frequently the result of a lawsuit recovery or settlement, or the disabled individual is a beneficiary of an estate or insurance policy. Since this book is intended as an estate planning guide, the following discussion will focus on the supplemental needs trust and will not include further discussions regarding the special needs trust.

THE SUPPLEMENTAL NEEDS TRUST

Estate planning for families with a child with disablilites requires special attention. One challenge is to provide benefits from the estate of the parents while at the same time, ensuring no loss of government benefits to their disabled son or daughter. Another major concern of the parents is who will take care of their child once they are gone. A supplemental needs trust is a trust arrangement established by parents (or others) to provide an inheritance for their disabled child to pay for his or her care and not have that inheritance diminish any government benefits available to the child.

The Benefits of a Supplemental Needs Trust

The supplemental needs trust has been developed in answer to the challenge that many families face in not being able to afford to provide for all of the needs of a disabled child. When faced with these expenses, parents will often utilize the services and benefits available from federal, state and local government programs. This allows the families to maintain family resources in case government programs would no longer be available for the child. Since many government benefits are paid only to needy recipients, a benefit of the supplemental needs trust is that it provides funds to supplement (but not supplant) the care provided by government benefits for the disabled child, and yet does not limit the ability of the child to receive government benefits.

HOW SUPPLEMENTAL NEEDS TRUSTS ARE ESTABLISHED

A supplemental needs trust may be established in the will or living trust of the parents or in a separate supplemental needs trust document.

The supplemental needs provision in the trust typically includes items not available through government benefits such as education, training and rehabilitation, companions or nursing aid services, recreation, entertainment and travel expenses.

The supplemental needs language must be carefully worded so that the principal and income of the trust is not permitted to be used for any benefit that could be paid for by government benefits. The issue is that if the trust is not written correctly, the government benefits will be denied until the trust is completely used up.

WHO SHOULD BE TRUSTEE?

The selection of trustee of a supplemental needs trust is of special importance. The trustee has two broad functions:

1. The administration of the trust assets relating to investment management decisions, tax reporting and gathering the income.
2. The duty to determine the amount and payee of distributions that need to be made to or for the benefit of the disabled child.

The trustee should not only be knowledgeable about the needs of the child, but also experienced in financial management. The pairing of a family member with a corporate trustee as co-trustees is a good combination for such trusts. The corporate trustee would manage the trust and its investments and the family member would make the decisions

Elements Required in a Supplemental Needs Trust Established in a Will or Revocable Living Trust

It is important that a number of factors be clearly addressed in a supplemental needs trust. As with the law regarding medical assistance, the law relating to supplemental needs trusts is constantly evolving. It is critical to consult with an attorney experienced with this very unique area of the law.

- The trust must clearly state that it is to "supplement, but not supplant government benefits to which the child may otherwise be entitled."
- The trust must specify that the grantor's intent is that after the death of the disabled child, specific individuals will receive the remainder in the trust, usually the siblings of the disabled child.
- The trust should identify the benefits that the disabled child is receiving or would be qualified to receive.
- The trust must not provide for distributions directly to the disabled child.
- The trust should give the trustee the authority to spend or accumulate income in the trustee's sole discretion.
- The trust should identify the state and its agencies as creditors prohibited from receiving distributions from the trust.
- The trust should have a spendthrift clause preventing the child from pledging trust assets as collateral for loans and preventing any creditors from acquiring trust assets.

regarding spending trust assets for the benefit of the disabled child. The individual family member co-trustee could also have the authority to change the corporate trustee, as well as the authority to hire experts.

HOW SUPPLEMENTAL NEEDS TRUSTS OPERATE

After the death of the one who established the trust (or immediately if the trust was funded during the grantor's lifetime), the trustee may distribute income and/or principal for the benefit of the child with the restriction that such distributions may only supplement and not replace government benefits to which the child is entitled. Upon the death of the child, the remaining trust assets must be payable to individuals other than the child's estate; this is usually the child's siblings. A supplemental needs trust is often named as the beneficiary of a life insurance policy that the parents may purchase on their own lives. This is a strategy employed to assure that the trust will have enough assets to care for the disabled child after the parents are gone.

Summary

Hopefully, this chapter has persuaded you that it is important to plan for possible incapacity. In the event of your incapacity, your needs fall into one of two broad categories, either managing your business or your health care requirements. You must be sure that you have identified the people that you want to handle your affairs. Although none of us can predict the future, there is a strong possibility that you or your spouse will eventually require skilled nursing care — either at home or in a nursing home. Planning for these costs now can greatly minimize the impact upon your estate. Planning for other family members that have disabilities has also been reviewed.

Part III

Who Will Receive Assets Upon Your Death?

"Life can only be understood backwards but it must be lived forward."

– Susan Kierbegaard

4

Using Wills & Trusts to Plan Your Estate

Topics Include

What Makes a Will Stand Up in Court?

The Eight Problems Solved by Wills

Choosing Your Executor

Gifts & Charities

Special Needs Considerations

Disadvantages of Wills

Various Types of Trusts

Introduction

IF YOU'VE READ THE EARLIER CHAPTERS, and not skipped ahead, you know that first you must approach estate planning with a knowledgeable team; then, you must ensure that non-probate assets have the beneficiary designations you intend align in practical terms with your will. Also, you understand the various types of ownership and what each means in terms of inheritance, and you have faced, steadfastly, the various issues surrounding incapacity. Now, on to the finer points of creating your will and the pros and cons of trusts.

The Will

A will is a unique legal document in that it does not become legally binding until the person who signed it dies. A chief purpose of a will is to communicate the wishes of the signer (TESTATOR for men and TESTATRIX for women) as to distribution of his or her assets upon death. Wills can be revoked by the testator at any time by destroying the original. The terms of an existing will can be amended by using a simple amendment known as a CODICIL.

The will increasingly has less influence over how your assets are distributed at death.

The will is the estate planning document that generally gets the most attention, but it increasingly has less influence over how your assets are distributed at death. Since assets can also pass at death by beneficiary designation, joint ownership, and trusts (collectively known as will substitutes), a will is only one of many means of controlling asset transfer at death. The explosive growth of annuities, IRAs and retirement plans which pass by beneficiary designation, creates the likelihood that ever fewer assets will be distributed by wills in the future.

What Makes It Legal?

INTENT

In order for a document to be considered a valid will, it must state that the one signing it intends it to be his or her will, and that it disposes of his or her assets at death.

CAPACITY

Even if the will is properly signed, there are two other requirements. One is that the person who signed it must be over eighteen years of age when it was signed. A second requirement is that the signer must have a sound mind when he or she signs it.

Being of Sound Mind...

One is considered to have the mental capacity to sign a will if they can comply with three requirements: (1) identify their family members; (2) have a basic understanding of the assets and possessions they own; and, (3) be able to form a plan for the distribution of their assets.

SIGNATURE

Pennsylvania is lenient regarding the legal requirements for signing a will. The law simply states that every will must be in writing and signed at the end of the document. Pennsylvania law does not require the presence of witnesses at the time a will is signed. Nevertheless, it is important to have witnesses present to ensure that the will can withstand possible challenges. These simple rules can be deceiving, and you should always consult a qualified estate planning attorney for assistance.

Pennsylvania law permits a self-proving will. Under this rule, the one signing the will does so in the presence of two witnesses. The two witnesses also sign the will stating that they were present when the will was signed, that the signer was over eighteen years of age, had a sound mind, and was not under duress. All signatures are then notarized. The benefit of the self-proving will is that the witnesses will not be required to appear at the register of wills office after the death of the testator. Wills that do not have this self-proving page attached will require the witnesses to sign a statement that they were present when the will was signed and that the signature is that of the one who made the will.

The Eight Primary Estate Planning Challenges Solved by Wills

Although the importance of the will has diminished in recent years because of the increased availability of other methods to distribute assets at death, a will provides benefits that make it a cornerstone of most estate plans. What follows are the eight primary estate planning challenges solved by wills.

1. CONTROL WHO RECEIVES YOUR ASSETS AFTER DEATH

Your will only controls assets that are titled in your name alone. These assets are known as your PROBATE ESTATE. Having a will to give direction where your assets will go after death means that you die testate. This is because you have written down your desires. To die and have no will means that you would die intestate. That means there is no writing stating your desires about the assets that were in your name alone. To die intestate means that your assets will be distributed according to state law, which could result in distributions to people you may not even know. At the least, intestacy could cause confusion and conflict among family members, since money and family can be a volatile combination.

To die and have no will means that your assets will be distributed according to state law.

Proper planning with a will helps assure security for a surviving spouse, parent, or children. By leaving an orderly plan of distribution through your will, you can be assured that your heirs will receive your assets according to your desires. Blended families that include children from a previous marriage especially benefit from this type of planning.

2. NAME YOUR OWN PERSONAL REPRESENTATIVE (EXECUTOR)

A will permits you to name the individual or institution you wish to carry out your instructions. In Pennsylvania, this person or institution is your PERSONAL REPRESENTATIVE. (Historically the term was EXECUTRIX for women and EXECUTOR for men.)

Responsibilities of a Personal Representative

1. Locate the will. (Make his job easier and tell him that he is the personal representative and where your will is located.)
2. Present the will to the register of wills at the county courthouse.
3. Locate and conserve assets (i.e. house, bank accounts, personal belongings, business, etc.). Note: Non-probate assets such as life insurance policies, 401(k) accounts and IRAs are not the responsibility of the personal representative.
4. Pay the debts and any claims against the estate.
5. Pay any taxes due.
6. Distribute the assets according to the will.

When choosing your personal representative, keep in mind that it can be one or more persons, a bank, or a trust company. A number of considerations apply when choosing the personal representative. The primary one should be the ability to do the job. Personal representatives generally hire an attorney to assist them; therefore, their skill may not be as important as trustworthiness. Typically, a husband and wife name each other as the personal representative and then name either adult children or a bank or a trust company as the successor personal representative. There are a number of advantages to naming a bank or a trust company as a personal representative. (*For a more detailed discussion concerning choosing trustees, see Chapter 5.*)

The personal representative is entitled to compensation that shall be "reasonable and just."

The personal representative is entitled to receive compensation for his duties and services provided. The law states that compensation to the personal representative shall be "reasonable and just."

If you are named the personal representative in someone else's will, keep in mind that you are *not* required to hire the attorney who wrote the will to assist you with estate settlement. As personal representative, you should use the attorney that you choose to best serve the estate. This attorney may or may not be the one who wrote the will.

Failure to name a personal representative will result in the court appointing an administrator to manage your estate. The administrator may be an individual or institution that you never used or met during your lifetime. Since you have the right to name an individual or a bank or a trust company to act as your personal representative, it is to your advantage to have a will prepared to do so.

3. "I'D TRUST YOU WITH MY FIRSTBORN." — NAME THE GUARDIAN FOR YOUR CHILDREN

Pennsylvania law permits the sole surviving parent of an unmarried minor child to appoint a GUARDIAN OF THE PERSON of such child to care for them until they reach age eighteen. A guardian of the person is the individual responsible for the day-to-day care of minor children, such as providing them with food, clothing, shelter and healthcare. Failure to have a will name a guardian of the person results in the court appointing the guardian. Family conflict could arise as numerous individuals may combat each other for the right to take care of the child. This would also incur additional costs for the legal assistance needed to have the court appoint a guardian.

You may appoint different guardians: one to care for your children (guardian of the person) and another to manage their money (GUARDIAN OF THE ESTATE). For example, you could name your sister as guardian over the care of your children and your father as guardian to manage their money. Take the initiative to name those individuals in your will who you prefer to care for the day-to-day needs of your minor children.

4. CONTROL WHEN YOUR CHILDREN, GRANDCHILDREN, OR OTHER HEIRS WILL RECEIVE THEIR INHERITANCE

As described in the preceding section, when a child under age eighteen receives an inheritance, and there is no provision made in a will or trust for its management, the court will determine how the inheritance will be managed. In many counties, the court will require that the inheritance must be deposited in a Pennsylvania bank, in a blocked account. This means that money can only be withdrawn from the account with a court order. Upon the minor's eighteenth birthday, the account will be closed and the minor will receive the entire inheritance. In the case of large estates, another option may be for the court to appoint a guardian of the estate.

"Not So Fast!"

Grandpa Wilson had founded a very successful chain of furniture stores, which he led with success and fanfare for forty years. He then sold the business and decided to create a trust to ensure money was there for the education and support of his grandchildren. He didn't want his daughter or her husband to have control of this fund. Nor did he want the inheritance to be handed to his grandchildren on their eighteenth birthdays. Grandpa Wilson knew the phrase "easy come, easy go," and he had some specific ideas about how his descendents should use their inheritance.

So, he specified that granddaughter Emily would receive $50,000 in trust to be used for college. If Emily decides she suddenly doesn't like the idea of higher education, the $50,000 would be held in trust until her thirtieth birthday at which time it would be dispersed in installments of $5,000 annually for as long as the assets lasted (as they would be invested to earn interest).

Grandpa Wilson's grandson, Mark, was also to receive $50,000. Mark had received a scholarship and didn't need money for college. His grandfather thought he might be good in business for himself, so he specified that Mark could use $25,000 of the total to start a business at age 30, with the remaining $25,000 alloted to him in annual payments. If he did not want to start a business, then he would receive the $50,000 in annual $5,000 payments like his sister.

5. Protect Your Heirs' Inheritance from Others

A will provides the flexibility to distribute your estate *immediately* to your heirs or maintain control by distributing it over a period of time through trusts. By maintaining your heirs' inheritance in trust, you can protect it in the event of their bankruptcy, lawsuits, and divorce settlements.

> Let's say Emily, in the previous example, does not go to college, but takes the $5,000 per year amount from the trust. By age 40, Emily is on her second marriage (and it's not going too well either) when she becomes the victim of a crime and dies. Now, Grandpa never intended for Husband Number Two to become the recipient of $5,000 per year for the rest of his life, and fortunately he made the appropriate provisions in his will. The money held in trust for Emily reverts to her brother Mark, who decides to fund a rose garden at the local park in his sister's honor because, while she didn't care for academics, she loved flowers and this was something Mark could do in her memory. Husband Number Two was surprised as he quickly learned the benefits one can utilize by establishing trusts in a will.

6. Turn Tax Dollars into Family Dollars

By using tax strategies in your will, you can save a significant portion of your estate from state and federal taxes. The chapters in this book discussing inheritance and estate taxes give specific directions outlining how to achieve these tax savings. (Failure to use federal estate tax strategies could result in needless taxes if your estate exceeds $1 million in 2002.) Using proper tax strategies can allow more money to pass to your beneficiaries.

Failure to use federal estate tax strategies in your will could result in needless taxes if your estate exceeds $1 million in 2002.

7. Give Gifts to Special People and Charities

Pennsylvanians contribute millions of dollars each year to charities. When planning their estates, however, they may overlook that without a will there are *no* distributions made to charities or anyone outside of one's family. This can mean a substantial loss of funds to close friends or charities.

If you contribute to the support of charities or special individuals, be sure to consider them when creating your estate plan. Otherwise, they may be left with nothing after you pass away. In addition, gifts to charities made through your will result in inheritance and estate tax deductions.

8. Protect Government Benefits of Family Members with Disabilities

As explained in Chapter 3, many families have children with disabilities that cause them to be dependent on others for assistance during their adult life. While their parents are living, such a child could live with them. Upon the death of the surviving parent, however, such children may require residential or nursing home services.

If a parent leaves an inheritance outright to a disabled child, the child would be required to fully consume his or her entire inheritance before qualifying for certain government benefits. With proper planning, the parents can make financial provision for such a child, while permitting him or her to receive government benefits. (*See page 62 for a list of the elements required in a supplemental needs trust established in a will or revocable living trust.*)

The Disadvantages of Wills

A will has no control in the event of your incapacity.

In spite of the eight primary solutions that wills provide, there are two distinct disadvantages: (1) A will only controls assets in your sole name. Since more and more assets are being passed to heirs outside a will, the plans so carefully laid out in your will never get a chance to control assets that are transferred at death (non-probate assets such as IRAs or annuities, for example). (2) Since your will only controls your assets in the event of your death, it has no control over your assets in the event of your incapacity.

Trusts

Trusts can provide important checks and balances for the management or distribution of your estate. They may offer several advantages as part of your overall estate plan. Taking the time and effort to establish a trust can relieve the anxiety you might feel when considering what would happen to your home, investments, business, minor children, elderly parents, spouse, or disabled children, should you become temporarily or permanently incapacitated. In the case of such an unfortunate situation, you will need all of your strength to concentrate on recovery. Therefore, it is wise and responsible to make decisions now that will keep everything running smoothly if the unforeseen happens. In many cases, only a trust will provide the planning opportunities needed to implement some of those decisions.

All trusts fall into one or more of the following catagories: IRREVOCABLE or REVOCABLE, and LIVING or TESTAMENTARY. Specific types of trusts are described in a number of different chapters within this book. Refer to the Index for the location of these various trusts. If a trust is established during the grantor's lifetime, it is known as a living trust, or INTER VIVOS trust. It will be either revocable or irrevocable. If a trust is established *after* the grantor's death, it is known as a TESTAMENTARY TRUST.

REVOCABLE LIVING TRUSTS

The distinguishing characteristic of a revocable living trust is that the grantor reserves the right to amend or revoke the trust at any time. This type of trust is also known for income tax purposes as a GRANTOR TRUST. This is because the IRS assigns the grantor's own social security number as the tax ID number of the trust so long as the grantor is also serving as the trustee. Hence, there is no requirement for a separate income tax return for the trust, so long as the grantor serves as the trustee and the trust is revocable. (*The revocable living trust is discussed at length in Chapter 5.*)

IRREVOCABLE LIVING TRUSTS

If the grantor decides to give up the right to revoke or amend the trust, he has established an irrevocable trust. These trusts are like lobster traps in that once the assets are put into the trust, they can *never* come back out. The primary reason that one would establish an irrevocable trust is to provide estate, income, or gift tax benefits to the grantor. Irrevocable trusts must have their own tax identification number and may be required to file tax returns.

The Basic Concept of a Trust

Assume that I wanted to give my daughter a $1,000 gift. I could simply write a check and hand it to her. The transaction would be completed. If I was uncomfortable with just handing her the money and wanted to have some strings attached to it, I could establish a trust by giving the money to my brother instead of directly to my daughter. I would give my brother instructions concerning how the money should be used to benefit my daughter. For example, I could write him a note and tell him that he can use the money to pay for her education or medical bills. I would not want him to give it to her so she could buy a Corvette or twenty-five pairs of shoes.

Instead of giving the gift directly to her, I have established a trust by giving the $1,000 to my brother to manage for my daughter's benefit. I am the grantor (or settlor) because I am the one that gave the money to my brother. My brother is the trustee because he is the one responsible to manage and distribute the money for my daughter's benefit. My daughter is the trust beneficiary because she is the one who receives the benefits of the money that is held in trust. The note I wrote to my brother is the trust agreement. This is the set of instructions that the grantor desires for the management of the money given to the trustee. The assets transferred into the trust are known as the principal or the corpus of the trust.

TESTAMENTARY TRUSTS

Although a trust may be designed and written during the grantor's lifetime (in a will for example), the plan may be that it is not established and funded until after the death of the grantor. This type of trust is a testamentary trust. Since these trusts do not exist until the death of the grantor, they are *always irrevocable*. These trusts are usually written into the grantor's will or living trust and are established to provide investment management and control over the distribution of trust assets.

Summary

Trusts can be as simple or as complex as the imagination or objectives of the grantor. Trusts are used in estate planning to provide benefits to the grantor by helping the grantor minimize or avoid taxation, maintain control over assets, and avoid probate. A number of specialized trusts will be discussed throughout this book.

5

Living Trusts in Pennsylvania

Topics Include

Living Trusts

The Eight Primary Challenges Solved by Living Trusts

The Operation & Tax Treatment of Living Trusts

Disadvantages of Living Trusts

Various Types of Living Trusts

Introduction

LIVING TRUSTS MAY BE THE MOST MISUNDERSTOOD of all estate planning documents. They are sold by telemarketers, direct mail, seminars and door-to-door salesmen. Unfortunately, this mass-marketing approach has resulted in more misunderstanding about living trusts than positive education. The role of the attorney on the

Secure the assistance of an attorney for the preparation of legal documents that affect assets.

estate planning team — one who is knowledgeable about living trusts — is critical when it comes to preparing living trusts. Every Pennsylvania resident is well advised to secure the assistance of a Pennsylvania attorney for the preparation of legal documents that affect their assets.

It is possible that a living trust is *not* to your advantage. There are many circumstances in which a well-crafted will and durable power of attorney will be sufficient, but only a qualified attorney should advise you on this matter.

This chapter will explain the benefits of living trusts. If a living trust is to be part of your estate plan, the various benefits we are about to discuss will motivate you to take action.

What Is a Revocable Living Trust?

A REVOCABLE LIVING TRUST is a legal document designed, created and signed by you while you are alive, hence the word "living." It is *revocable* because you are reserving the power to revoke it at any time.

The Eight Primary Estate Planning Challenges Solved by Living Trusts

1. "The Hub of the Wheel" — A Living Trust-Centered Estate Plan Creates a Master Plan to Control the Distribution of All Your Assets in the Event of Your Death

Envision for a moment a wagon wheel, spokes extending outward. If the wheel represents your estate plan, with the spokes the various assets (your home, annuities, life insurance, etc.), then the hub represents the living trust. A well-constructed, comprehensive living trust is the hub of your estate plan, and all assets and property are brought under the control of one managing document — a document that is able to legally operate, relatively seamlessly, beyond your lifetime. With the living trust-centered estate plan, all of your assets and property are brought into one master plan. In effect, the living trust sweeps all probate and most non-probate assets under the authority of just one document. The living trust is a significant tool that can provide a comprehensive estate plan for your assets during your lifetime and after death.

The comprehensive nature of living trusts ensures continuity and agreement among the various assets of your estate and how they are handled. Instead of assets being distributed by different plans set up at different times by different advisors, the living trust provides one comprehensive estate plan for the management and distribution of all your assets. This assures that your plans are carried out in an orderly, secure manner.

> Life insurance proceeds (not payable to the estate) are non-probate assets, and as such, are not controlled by your will. They are paid directly from the insurance company to the beneficiary named in the policy. By establishing a living trust during your lifetime (and directing that the life insurance benefits be paid to the trustee of your revocable living trust), the proceeds will be fully controlled by your trust after death and still avoid probate. This arrangement permits you to pay the proceeds outright to your loved ones or to have the proceeds managed for their benefit. The living trust affords the opportunity for you to address the needs of your family in a more personal manner.

Living trusts can ensure that life insurance proceeds are handled exactly as you wish; they can also prevent accidental disinheritance, a result of joint ownership discussed in Chapter 2. In short, the directions in the trust may be tailored to meet the specific needs of your loved ones.

Another benefit of living trusts is that investments registered as T.O.D. (transfer on death) can also be paid directly to your living trust to be a part of your comprehensive estate plan and still avoid probate.

2. The "Oh No! What Now?" Factor — A Living Trust Avoids Court Control of Your Assets in Case of Incapacity

One of the reasons people establish an estate plan is so their wishes are carried out with regard to the guardianship of their minor children, and to confirm the control of their own assets in the event of their death or if they become incapacitated. A well-crafted living trust will address the latter issue by naming a SUCCESSOR TRUSTEE. If a living trust is in place, with a successor trustee named, then there is no need for the court to appoint a guardian to control your assets if you become incapacitated. Not only will the court not control the management of your assets, but *your instructions in the living trust will prevail.*

Your living trust continues to control your assets if you become incapacitated because the living trust owns the assets, not you.

> Bill was the successful owner of an investment company. A hands-on entrepreneur, he managed the firm's largest portfolios, and his attention to his business and the business world around him was pervasive and nonstop.
>
> One unfortunate evening, he was involved in a car accident. He survived, but sustained a severe concussion and his legs suffered extensive trauma. He would return to his business, but the rehabilitation was going to be lengthy. Bill's family, employees and clients were depending on him, but he had to concentrate on getting well.
>
> Fortunately, the previous year Bill had taken the time to establish a living trust as part of his estate plan. The successor trustee Bill chose was his father, who had been his mentor and was now retired. Bill, Sr. was legally able to step in and manage his son's financial affairs while Bill and his wife and children concentrated on recovery.

What about Your Power of Attorney?

Although the agent you named in your power of attorney has authority to act on your behalf, your agent is not *required* to act. Your successor trustee, however, has a duty to act for your benefit. In addition, the power of attorney may not contain specific instructions regarding your individual desires. The power of attorney contains a list of activities that the agent has your permission to engage in, but it cannot elaborate all of your intentions for yourself and your loved ones. The trustee of your living trust does have specific instructions from you so he or she knows exactly what to do to fulfill your desires. It is important to keep in mind that even those with living trusts should always also have a power of attorney. It will be required to manage assets not held by the trust.

Even those with living trusts should always also have a power of attorney to manage assets not held by the trust.

3. "TIME IS MONEY" — A LIVING TRUST SAVES TIME & MONEY WHEN SETTLING YOUR ESTATE

Assets registered in the name of your living trust are not probate assets and therefore avoid court administration. It is often *less costly* to settle your estate when your assets are registered in the name of a living trust. This is because you register your assets in the name of your living trust during your lifetime. Registration to the living trust can simplify the distribution process at your death. Your heirs need not wait for your executor to re-register and transfer the assets. Registering assets in the name of your trust during lifetime should result in lower attorney's fees after death and will also avoid executor's fees on assets registered to your living trust. It is important to realize, however, that your successor trustee must have the knowledge and ability to administer your trust and distribute your assets. In the absence of such knowledge, the successor trustee will need to hire the services of a lawyer or CPA to help finalize your affairs. Give careful consideration to your selection of a successor trustee.

You may have read that there will be no "last expenses" if you use a living trust, but this is not true.

For the purpose of discussion assume that the attorney's fees for settling a particular estate would be approximately five percent of the value of assets that were in the decedent's name. Assets registered in the name of a living trust, however, are non-probate assets and, therefore, the attorney's fees for helping to close the same estate that had used a living trust could be as low as one to one and one-half percent. This is a savings of three and one-half to four percent of the value of the estate. You may have read that there will be no last expenses if you use a living trust, but this is *not* true. Even with a living trust, there may still be the need to file a Pennsylvania inheritance tax return and a final income tax return. There may also be expenses such as appraisals related to the value of real estate and other assets which must be included in death tax returns.

Assets registered in the name of a living trust can usually be transferred to the beneficiaries after the grantor's death faster than if the assets were to pass through probate. The successor trustee has immediate access to living trust assets because the successor trustee does not have to engage in the activity of locating your will, probating it and petitioning the register of wills to issue a short certificate.

> A living trust may help avoid probate proceedings in other states as well. Real estate owned outside Pennsylvania is subject to the probate laws of that state. For example, if you owned shore property in New Jersey, the state of New Jersey will require probate proceedings to transfer the ownership of that property to the name of your heirs. If you re-titled your property into the name of your living trust, it would not be required to go through New Jersey probate, although it may require payment of New Jersy inheritance tax.

4. "Stand by Your Plan" — A Living Trust Provides Lifetime Management of a Grantor's Assets

A living trust provides standby professional investment management in the event of your incapacity or prolonged absence. A STANDBY LIVING TRUST is established by naming a bank or trust company as your successor trustee. In such case, if you leave the country for extended travel or should become incapacitated, you know that there will be continuity in the management of your assets. Also, unlike the power of attorney, the management will be according to your specific directions. Using a standby living trust provides greater assurance that your investments will be professionally managed by the bank or trust company you named until you regain capacity or return to the country.

5. "KEEPING ASSETS WARM" — A LIVING TRUST PROVIDES CONTINUITY OF ASSET MANAGEMENT

Another benefit of living trusts is the continuity they offer upon your death. Remember, although you may (and should) include a power of attorney in your estate plan, this power ends at your death. All of your property and assets are frozen until a personal representative (executor) is appointed and a short certificate is issued by the register of wills. The short certificate provides the personal representative the authority to manage your assets. Since a living trust continues after your death, no such freezing is required. As a result, your investments may continue to be actively managed as they were during your lifetime.

> If federal estate tax planning is a part of your estate plan, establishing a living trust assures that assets are transferred into the credit shelter trust of the first spouse to die. Once your living trust is established, it is important to register into the name of the living trust the assets that are planned to become a part of the credit shelter trust after your death. The benefit is that your successor trustee will not be required to make any changes to your investments and could automatically become the trustee of your credit shelter trust. The credit shelter trustee will, however, be required to have a new IRS Tax ID number assigned to the credit shelter trust. This strategy is for an estate plan requiring mandatory funding of the credit shelter trust. (*Credit shelter trusts are covered in detail in Chapter 8. For a discussion on mandatory funding versus disclaimer funding of credit shelter trusts, see Chapter 9.*)

Another benefit of continuity is that your successor trustee often has access to your trust assets quicker than the personal representative would have authority over assets in your name alone.

6. "HOLES IN THEIR POCKETS" SYNDROME — A LIVING TRUST CAN CONTROL THE DISTRIBUTION OF BENEFITS

Your living trust may direct that it immediately pays out to all your beneficiaries their inheritance. On the other hand, as mentioned earlier, you also have the option to control the timing of distributions to your heirs. Parents often desire that children receive their inheritance over a number of years. For example, one-third at age twenty-one, one-third at age twenty-five and the balance at age thirty. The successor trustee, under such a plan, would continue to manage the trust assets and make distributions for health and education needs.

7. "SEE YA IN COURT, SISTER!" — A LIVING TRUST REDUCES THE RISK OF LITIGATION

The enforceability of a living trust is not totally dependent upon the grantor's state of mind at the time the trust was signed.

Family conflict may be minimized by providing specific instructions in your living trust concerning the disposition of your assets. This is an excellent way to plan your estate if you suspect there may be some family conflict after you are gone. Living trusts are more difficult to overturn than wills. Will contests are frequently based upon allegations of mental confusion on the part of the testator. Was she incapacitated? Was she under duress?

One major distinction between a will and a living trust is that the enforceability of a living trust is not totally dependent upon the grantor's state of mind at the time the trust was signed. Since a living trust becomes legally binding when it is signed, and is used over time after it is signed, it is far more difficult to overturn. A living trust, by its very nature, shows careful consideration on the part of grantor; registering assets into the name of your trust is additional evidence that you had all your capacities at the time you signed your trust. In addition, your use of your living trust before your death makes it less subject to any type of contest.

8. "No One Needs To Know You Left Everything to the Teddy Bear Museum" — A Living Trust Provides More Privacy Than Probate

Everyone's will is open to public inspection after death. When newspapers report the gifts made to charities from estates, it is the result of a reporter reading wills at the courthouse. A living trust is not a public document filed at the register of wills office in the courthouse. As a result, the trust is not available to the public.

To protect the living trust as a private document, send the trust under separate cover.

Unfortunately, in many counties in Pennsylvania, the Pennsylvania inheritance tax return is subject to public review. The tax return lists the names of all the estate's beneficiaries and the inheritance each received. In spite of this, there is some added privacy with a living trust. The inheritance tax return does not indicate the exact timing of distributions to heirs. In addition, other personal family information in a living trust is not open to public review. Another privacy concern is the fact that the Pennsylvania inheritance tax return requires a copy of a living trust to be attached to it when the return is filed at the register of wills office. In order to protect the living trust as a private document, it is possible to send the living trust under separate cover to the department of revenue in Harrisburg at the time the inheritance tax return is filed.

How Revocable Living Trusts Operate

Grantor

The person who creates the living trust is known as the GRANTOR. The grantor transfers assets to the trustee of the trust to be controlled by the trustee.

Trustee

The TRUSTEE is named by the grantor when the living trust is established. The grantor usually names himself or herself as the original trustee and manages living trust assets for his or her own benefit and the benefit of others according to the instructions in the trust agreement. The living trust usually permits the original trustee to be removed and replaced by the grantor as long as the grantor is alive and not incapacitated.

SUCCESSOR TRUSTEE

The SUCCESSOR TRUSTEE continues to manage the living trust assets if the original trustee dies, resigns, or becomes incapacitated.

BENEFICIARY

The primary BENEFICIARY of a living trust is usually the grantor. Again, the grantor often serves as the trustee. Upon the death of the grantor/trustee, the successor trustee assumes management authority. The living trust usually directs that upon the death of the grantor, the trust assets should be distributed to the beneficiaries named in the trust agreement.

How to Choose a Trustee

Remember, a power of attorney is not required to act, but a trustee has a duty, in fact a number of duties, assigned to him or her by law. The trustee must follow the directions written in the living trust by the grantor and is responsible to manage the trust assets *according to the terms of the trust.* The trustee also has a duty of loyalty to the trust and to the grantor. This means that the trustee cannot act in any way to harm the trust or grantor.

Duties of the Trustee

- Collect and control trust assets
- Preserve trust assets
- Deal impartially with all beneficiaries
- Keep trust assets separate
- Enforce and defend any claims and actions against the trust
- Report and pay all state and federal taxes owed by the trust

WHO CAN BE YOUR TRUSTEE?

You, the grantor, can serve as the original trustee (or you and your spouse as co-trustees). The grantor usually serves as the original trustee of his or her living trust. Adult children may also serve as trustees or successor trustees. One child could serve alone or two or more could serve together as co-trustees.

Banks or trust companies are generally chosen by grantors who do not have the time, ability or desire to manage their own assets.

Banks or trust companies may also be appointed to serve alone or as co-trustees with an individual that you name. Banks or trust companies are generally chosen by grantors who do not have the time, ability or desire to manage their own assets. There are a number of advantages to naming banks or trust companies. They are permanent. They don't die or move away. Such trustees are also financially accountable; you can always rest assured that state and federal examiners are watching the activities of banks and trust companies. In addition, banks and trust companies are impartial and experienced and provide professional investment management.

Individual trustees, on the other hand, serve under the honor system. There is no government agency looking over their shoulders to make sure that they are wise in the administration of your trust. People often choose individuals to serve as trustee because they may not charge a fee. In addition, individual trustees may have personal interest and knowledge of the beneficiaries and their special situations, or may have more specific investment or business expertise regarding unique trust assets. The selection of the trustee is vital to the viability of your estate plan. It merits careful thought and should not be taken lightly.

SUCCESSOR TRUSTEES

When the grantor/trustee dies or becomes incapacitated, the successor trustee steps in to manage the trust assets. The same considerations regarding naming the trustee apply to naming your successor trustee. Who is best suited to serve as your successor trustee? Every situation is unique. There is no simple answer. You must weigh the pro's and con's of naming an individual as your successor trustee or naming a bank or trust company.

The Registration Process (Funding Your Living Trust)

It is not enough to create a living trust defining your objectives, naming your trustee and successor trustee and specifying how you would like your estate managed and distributed upon your death. You *must transfer your assets* from your sole name into your name as trustee of your trust. Once this is done you no longer own your assets, the trust does. You do not lose control of your assets, however, because you control the trust and can revoke or change it at any time. The trust only controls assets that are titled in its name, so transferring should be done immediately.

Transfer the Following Assets into Your Living Trust

- CDs
- Bank accounts
- Stocks and bonds
- Real estate
- Business assets
- Mutual funds

Immediately after signing your trust, you, as grantor, will engage in this registration process. Upon your death, any assets not registered in the name of your trust during your lifetime will be re-registered into the name of your trust by your executor, because your pour-over will pours all such assets over into your living trust to then be controlled by the successor trustee named in your living trust.

How to Re-Register Assets into the Name of Your Living Trust: A Step-by-Step Guide

The following is an example of titling assets into an individual living trust: "John Q. Public, Trustee of the John Q. Public Revocable Living Trust dated February 13, 2002." For married couples establishing a joint trust, the title would be: "John Q. Public and Jane Q. Public, Trustees of the John Q. Public and Jane Q. Public Revocable Living Trust dated February 13, 2002."

> During the process of transferring your assets into your living trust, someone may ask for the trust's tax identification number. You must use your own social security number for this purpose. The trust will not pay taxes or even file a tax return so long as you, the grantor, are trustee. You will pay taxes on the income earned by your trust on your personal 1040 federal income tax return and your Pennsylvania state income tax return.

REAL ESTATE

A deed is required to re-title your real estate into the name of your living trust. Re-titling real estate into your living trust raises four issues that must be considered:

1. **The Pennsylvania Realty Transfer Tax:** The Pennsylvania realty transfer tax may be required to be paid on such a transfer. There is an exemption from the realty transfer tax for conveyances into a living trust. However, the transfer tax law narrowly defines what a living trust is and it does not necessarily include a trust simply because it calls itself a living trust. The exact language of the trust must be carefully reviewed to confirm that no transfer taxes would be due upon transferring your real estate into your trust.

2. **The due on sale clause on a mortgage secured by the real estate:** Due on sale clauses in existing mortgages must also be given careful consideration before recording a new deed. These types of provisions in mortgages protect the lender from the borrower transferring the real estate, still keeping it subject to the mortgage, without first seeking the permission of the lender. If an unauthorized transfer of the real estate occurs, the due on sale clause in the mortgage may require the entire mortgage to be immediately paid in full. Mortgage lenders are not allowed to invoke the due on sale clause if the grantor of a living trust lives in his or her home and transfers the home in which he lives to a living trust. Therefore, on your personal residence, there is no concern with the due on sale clause in the mortgage document.

> If the property being transferred into the trust is not occupied by the owner of the real estate, or if it is commercial real estate, the best practice is to notify the lender before transferring the real estate and obtain written assurances from the lender that the due on sale clause would not be enforced. Another reason to notify the mortgage lender before transferring real estate into a trust is that some lenders may require that the mortgage be re-written naming the trustee as the mortgagor.

3. **Notifying your homeowners or property casualty insurance company to list your trust as a loss payee:** It is also important to notify the homeowners or property casualty insurance company when transferring real estate into a trust and have them issue a confirmation that the conveyance has not disturbed any insurance coverage.
4. **Impact on owner's title insurance coverage should be considered:** Because numerous title companies are writing owner's coverage in Pennsylvania, there are a number of different positions taken regarding the effect on owner's title coverage due to

the conveyance of the real estate into a living trust. If continued title insurance owner's coverage in the real estate is important, contact the title company that wrote the owner's coverage and follow the procedures they recommend.

BANK ACCOUNTS

If you fund a living trust with your bank accounts, you must sign a new signature card for your accounts. You will register the assets into the name of your trust. Generally, a customer account representative at your bank can help you make this change. Some banks may require that you close an existing account and open a new one. If you do open a new account, be sure not to close the old one right away. Remember, closing out an account will affect any direct deposits received by that account. Wait until you have changed any direct deposits to go into the new account and wait until the new account receives at least one deposit.

BANK CDS

Banks charge a penalty for early withdrawal of a certificate of deposit (CD). This may also apply to changing the registration of your CD into a living trust. Some banks, however, will waive the penalty if the transfer is going into a living trust. Since the trust maintains the same tax ID number (your social security number), there is no change in the taxable entity, only the title on the CD. If your bank will not waive the penalty, you must decide whether it would be better for you to transfer the CDs now and pay the penalty, or wait and transfer the CDs into your trust after they mature.

By simply re-registering the name on a brokerage account, you can move all of your investments in the account into your living trust.

STOCKS, BONDS & MUTUAL FUNDS

To transfer stocks, bonds or mutual funds that you hold in a brokerage account into your trust, you need only re-register the name of the account to your trust. This is done by changing the registration of the account from your name alone into your name as trustee of your trust. Your broker or financial advisor can assist you with this. Brokerage accounts are the easiest vehicles to transfer because by simply re-registering the name on a brokerage account, you can move all of your investments in the account into your living trust.

If you own stocks or bonds in your name and hold the certificates, you will have to deal directly with the corporation or the borrower. Simply call the phone number that appears with the information you receive with your dividends. Tell the transfer agent that you wish to have them mail you the documents necessary to re-register your investments into another name. This is a simple process. Every corporation has its own unique paperwork; however, just ask them to mail the appropriate forms and follow their instructions.

LIFE INSURANCE

Change the beneficiary of your life insurance to your trust by securing a change of beneficiary form from your life insurance agent.

IRAS & QUALIFIED RETIREMENT PLANS

IRAs and most qualified retirement plans permit the surviving spouse to roll over the deceased spouse's IRA or qualified retirement plan into their own plan.

It may not be in your best interest to name your living trust the beneficiary of any IRAs or qualified retirement plans you own. Such a decision could cause unwanted tax consequences. Before acting, you should discuss these beneficiary designations with your attorney, CPA or your plan administrator to determine the alternatives available to you and the potential tax consequences. This consultation should be done before making any changes to these plans.

The reason for the possible unwanted tax consequence is that IRAs and most qualified retirement plans permit the surviving spouse to roll over the deceased spouse's IRA or qualified retirement plan into their own plan. In other words, if husband names his wife the beneficiary of his IRA, at husband's death, his wife simply takes ownership of the IRAs and continues the income tax deferral. If someone other than his wife were to be beneficiary of such tax-deferred investments, there may be different income tax results. (*See Chapter 6 for a more detailed discussion of IRAs and qualified retirement plans.*)

The Operation of the Revocable Living Trust

Trusts offer control by clearly stating what happens to your assets.

Once you have completed the registration process, your living trust is now prepared to provide maximum benefits. Since the trust owns the assets registered in its name, the trust document offers a CONTINUUM OF CONTROL by clearly stating what happens to your assets no matter what happens to you.

While You Are Healthy

You transfer title of your assets into the name of the living trust and keep complete control over all trust assets while you are healthy.

If You Become Incapacitated

In the trust you have named your successor trustee to step in and administer the assets of the trust in case you become incapacitated. Once you regain your capacity, your successor trustee will step down, and you will once again resume control as trustee. The successor trustee will only administer the trust while you are incapacitated.

In the Event of Your Death

The executor you named in your will is instructed to pour-over your assets into your trust. Debts will be paid and assets will be distributed by your successor trustee as you have specified in the trust document. Sometimes the pour-over will instructs that debts and expenses are to be paid from the probate estate prior to distribution to the trust. The trust identifies all beneficiaries to receive the assets upon your death, which would include family, charity and friends.

Tax Treatment of Revocable Living Trusts

A living trust is known as a GRANTOR TRUST because the trust's tax ID number is the same as the grantor's social security number. As a result, all tax events of the trust are reported on the grantor's personal income tax return. Therefore, so long as the grantor is serving as the trustee, the IRS does not require a separate tax return for the trust. When a bank or trust company serves as trustee, a separate tax ID number is required.

> As a grantor trust, there are no income tax advantages unique to a revocable living trust. There are certain inheritance and estate tax benefits that can be written into the living trust, but these same provisions could be written into a will and are, therefore, not unique to living trusts.

Disadvantages of Living Trusts

Despite all of the discussion and articles concerning the benefits of living trusts they do have a number of disadvantages.

1. "A Penny Saved..." — A Living Trust Is More Expensive Than a Will To Establish

The legal fees for husband and wife for a living trust-centered estate plan can be significantly higher than the fee for a will. This higher expense may be justified by greater benefits, but one cannot deny that the initial expense of living trusts is higher than wills. Even with a living trust, a will is still necessary to provide the pour-over benefits to sweep into the living trust assets that were not registered in the name of the trust during the grantor's life.

2. "Details ... Details ..." — Living Trusts Are More Complex

The living trust must be "funded" by re-registering titles and beneficiary designations of all your investments to bring them under the control of the trust. Some people find this activity to be burdensome and not worth the effort. Living trusts can be amended by simply adding one- or two-page amendments to the existing trust. If one has a completely new living trust prepared, it might require going through the entire registration process again.

3. "TUNNEL VISION" — A FOCUS ON PROBATE AVOIDANCE IGNORES OTHER ISSUES

Concentrating only on avoiding probate can cause one to ignore other significant issues in the overall estate plan.

Many people believe that simply having a living trust completes their estate planning. A fixation on probate avoidance can cause one to ignore deeper tax planning or family issues in the estate plan.

4. "TIME'S UP!" — A LOSS OF STATUTORY DEADLINE FOR CREDITOR'S CLAIMS

One advantage of the probate process is that creditors must file claims against the estate of a deceased person within one year of the publication of the notice that the decedent has died. If one has his or her entire estate titled in the name of a living trust, and no one publishes the fact that the grantor has died, there is no statutory cutoff regarding the time that a creditor may have to bring a claim against the grantor's estate. The result is that a creditor could potentially bring a claim against the estate many years after death and attempt to collect the debt from the trust beneficiaries.

In order to cut off the claims of creditors against the estate of a decedent, many attorneys will still probate the pour-over will and publish the fact that a grantor is deceased. (*See page 98.*) Also, the living trust does not give protection from the claims of creditors during lifetime.

Types of Living Trusts & Related Estate Planning Documents

JOINT TRUSTS

Joint trusts are trusts wherein husband and wife serve as co-grantors, co-trustees and co-primary beneficiaries while they are living. At the death of the first spouse, the surviving spouse continues as the surviving trustee, grantor and primary beneficiary. After the death of the second spouse the successor trustee will step in and distribute the trust assets to the beneficiaries.

CREDIT SHELTER TRUSTS

Couples using credit shelter trusts should have individual living trusts with plans related to the federal estate tax.

When a husband and wife are planning for the federal estate tax (*covered in detail in Chapter 9*), they will each have their own separate living trust with a CREDIT SHELTER TRUST written inside. The reason that husband and wife each have their own living trust is that in order to fund the credit shelter trust when the first spouse dies, the assets used to fund the credit shelter trust should be in the sole name (either outright or in trust) of the deceased grantor.

There are a number of states other than Pennsylvania where it is permissible for husband and wife to be co-trustees of a joint trust that would have credit shelter trust language inside. This arrangement is risky in Pennsylvania as there is the possibility that the assets in a joint trust would be seen as joint assets owned by husband and wife and would cause needless confusion related to the capability of funding the credit shelter trust with jointly owned assets. The more predominant practice in Pennsylvania is for husband and wife each to have their own separate living trust if the trust contains plans related to the federal estate tax. Nevertheless, there are some attorneys in Pennsylvania who do utilize a joint trust with credit shelter provisions. In such cases, they also have the clients sign a tenancy agreement, which is intended to change joint tenancy assets into tenancy in common.

Documents That Should Accompany Living Trusts

THE POUR-OVER WILL

This is a brief will that appoints the personal representative of the estate and gives instructions to transfer any assets into the trust if the grantor did not do so during the grantor's lifetime. Assets going into the living trust by way of the POUR-OVER WILL must go through the probate process.

DURABLE POWER OF ATTORNEY

This is the document that gives control to another person (your agent) in the event you are incapacitated or unavailable. A power of attorney can be immediate or springing. An immediate power of attorney is one giving the power and authority to your agent to act in your name immediately upon signing the document. A springing power of attorney is one where your agent cannot serve until you have been certified incapacitated by the court or by a physician.

Assets going into the living trust by way of the pour-over will must go through the probate process.

LIVING WILL

Living will documents quite often accompany the living trust in a revocable living trust-centered estate plan. (*See Chapter 3 for a detailed discussion of living wills.*)

Summary

The living trust is a versatile and beneficial estate planning document that should be considered by most people establishing their estate plan. In particular, the living trust should be considered by those who:

- Own real estate in states outside of Pennsylvania;
- Own multiple properties inside Pennsylvania;
- Have estates over $1,000,000 requiring federal estate tax planning;
- Feel that there is a potential for family conflict within their families after their death; or,
- Desire to benefit from one of the eight primary benefits of living trusts covered in this chapter.

As you can see, probate avoidance is not the only reason to give the living trust serious consideration but is only one of many benefits that this estate planning tool can provide.

6

Estate Planning for Retirement Plans & IRAs

Topics Include

The Basic Types of Retirement Plans

Taxes That Affect Retirement Plans & IRAs

Retirement Plan Distributions during Lifetime & after Death

Naming Retirement Plan Beneficiaries

Introduction

ON JANUARY 11, 2001 THE IRS ISSUED new proposed minimum distribution regulations regarding distributions from qualified retirement plans and IRAs. These new proposed regulations make significant changes to the existing regulations and provide for a far more simple and uniform method for calculating required distributions from retirement plans.

The main cause for the growth in these plans — income tax deferral — is also the main cause of confusion.

As of 2000, the U.S. Census Bureau reported 2,294,000 Pennsylvanians age 45 to 59 and 1,462,000 between the ages of 60 and 74. Due to the aging of Pennsylvanians, the amount of money contributed to retirement plans has increased significantly over the last five years. For many, their qualified retirement plan or individual retirement account (IRA) is their largest investment. It is ironic that the main cause for the growth in these plans — income tax deferral — is also the main cause of confusion concerning estate planning for qualified retirement plans and IRAs. The rules and regulations relating to retirement plans are complex. The EMPLOYEE RETIREMENT INCOME SECURITY ACT OF 1974 (ERISA) is the federal law covering pensions and other retirement programs. In addition to retirement plans governed by ERISA, there are traditional IRAs, Roth IRAs, 401(k) plans and 403(b) plans, among others.

Review Your Qualified Retirement Plan

In order to confirm the rules and regulations that govern your retirement plan, you must review your plan as well as your beneficiary designations.

QUALIFIED RETIREMENT PLANS

A qualified retirement plan is one in which the employer is entitled to an income tax deduction when contributions are made to the plan. This is permitted even if the employee is *not* required to include the amount as taxable income. The employer establishes the plan and determines the rights and opportunities of the participants, subject to IRS regulations. There are two broad types of qualified retirement plans: the defined benefit plan and the defined contribution plan.

A defined benefit plan is a qualified retirement plan that provides for a fixed benefit upon retirement. The amount of the benefit is specified in the plan; usually it is calculated as a percentage of the earnings of the participant over a period of time.

A more popular type of qualified retirement plan is the defined contribution plan. In this plan the employer and/or employee contributes a

Basic Types of Retirement Plans

1. Qualified Retirement Plans
   a. The defined benefit plan: provides for a fixed payment plan upon retirement; benefits are specified in the plan and are usually a percentage of the participant's earnings
   b. The defined contribution plan: the employer may contribute a specified amount to the plan each year. The 401(k) is the most familiar defined contribution plan
2. Individual Retirement Accounts (IRA): an individual's savings program with tax-deferred growth
   a. Traditional IRAs: contributions are tax deductable
   b. Roth IRAs: contributions are non-deductible

specified amount throughout the year. The employer's contribution to the plan may or may not be fixed. The most familiar defined contribution plan is the 401(k) plan, where the participant elects to have a certain percentage of his compensation contributed to the plan. The amounts contributed to the plan are deferred from the participant's taxable federal income.

Many employers match a portion of the participant's contribution to the 401(k). In several plans, the participants have some input into how contributions are allocated among investment options offered by the plan administrator.

TRADITIONAL INDIVIDUAL RETIREMENT ACCOUNTS (IRAS)

An IRA is essentially an individual's savings program with tax-deferred growth. IRAs are different than qualified retirement plans in a number of ways, and one must keep in mind that what is true for an IRA is not necessarily the same for a qualified retirement plan. The rules regarding IRAs are found in Internal Revenue Code §408, and it is easy to make generalizations about them. One must keep in mind, however, that what is true for an IRA is not necessarily the same for a qualified retirement plan; they are different in a number of ways. Most of the following discussion on IRAs concerns traditional IRAs.

ROTH IRAs

The Taxpayer Relief Act of 1997 gave us a new type of IRA known as a ROTH IRA. There are a number of differences between the Roth IRA and the traditional IRA. One significant difference is that contributions to Roth IRAs are *not* income tax deductible. The benefit, however, is that distributions from Roth IRAs are generally not taxable as income.

Contributions

- Contributions to a Roth IRA are not income tax deductible
- The maximum contribution for Roth IRAs is the same as that for traditional IRAs:

  1. For 2002 through 2004, it is $3,000.
  2. For 2005 through 2007, the maximum amount rises to $4,000.
  3. For 2008, the maximum contribution reaches $5,000.
  4. The amount one can contribute to a Roth IRA is phased out for single taxpayers beginning with income over $95,000, or $150,000 for married taxpayers.

Income Tax-Free Withdrawals

Roth IRA contributions can be withdrawn at any time *without any restrictions, taxes or penalties whatsoever.* Distributions of earnings from Roth IRAs are not included in income under certain situations:

- You must be at least $59^1/_2$ years old and,
- You must have held the account for a minimum of five years.

(There are exceptions to this rule based on death, disability, or for first-time homebuyers.)

- There is no requirement to start withdrawing money when you reach age 70½. In fact, you can continue to make contributions after that age. (This is the most significant difference between Roth IRAs and traditional IRAs.)

Penalty-Free Withdrawals

The penalty-free withdrawals for the Roth IRA are the same as that for the traditional IRA:

- Up to $10,000 for first-time homebuyers, and
- Unlimited for certain education purposes or death or disability.

Due to the unique features of the Roth IRA, the rest of the discussions of this chapter will be referring only to the traditional IRA and not the Roth IRA.

Taxes Affecting Qualified Retirement Plans & IRAs

Taxes must be carefully considered when making decisions about lifetime distributions from retirement plans or choosing retirement plan beneficiaries. The following are some tax traps to be aware of:

When distributions are received before the participant is 59½ years old, there is a 10% penalty.

10% Penalty Tax on Plan Distributions Taken Too Soon

When distributions are received from retirement plans or traditional IRAs before the participant is 59½ years old, there is a 10% penalty on the amount received. In addition to the penalty, income tax is due on the amount withdrawn from the retirement plan.

The 10% penalty does *not* apply if the distribution is made because of the death or total disability of the participant or to make medical payments on his or her behalf. It also does not apply for qualified education expenses or for limited amounts used for a first-time home purchase. In addition, the penalty does *not* apply if the amount withdrawn is rolled over into another IRA or qualified retirement plan within sixty days of taking the distribution. There is also an exemption from the 10% penalty for substantially equal periodic payments. This is a withdrawal system in which the IRA is depleted by taking substantially equal payments over the lifetime of the participant and a designated beneficiary.

The required beginning date is April 1 following the year in which the participant reaches age 70½.

50% Penalty Tax on Plan Distributions Not Taken Soon Enough

All qualified retirement plans and traditional IRAs require the participant to begin receiving distributions from the plan no later than his required beginning date (RBD). The required beginning date is April 1 of the calendar year following the year in which the participant reaches age 70½.

The IRS has tables that establish life expectancy factors to be used by participants to determine the minimum distribution required to be received from the retirement plan or IRA. If the minimum distribution is not received, a penalty of 50% is imposed on the difference between the actual distribution received and the minimum distribution required.

Income Tax (Income in Respect of a Decedent)

After the participant's death, if a beneficiary receives a distribution from the retirement plan or IRA, the distribution is taxable income to the beneficiary (at the beneficiary's tax rate) as income in respect of a decedent. If the proceeds are payable to the participant's estate, the entire amount is taxed at the estate's income tax rate. If the distribution is payable to the participant's surviving spouse, he or she may elect to roll over the distribution into a new IRA thereby avoiding tax due to income in respect of decedent and continuing to defer the income tax.

This rule is based on the fact that during the participant's lifetime, the assets in the retirement plan were not taxed. Therefore, after death, whoever inherits the retirement plan is required to pay the income tax. For this reason, retirement plans are only tax deferred, not tax exempt.

FEDERAL ESTATE TAX

The value of retirement plans and IRAs owned by the participant are subject to the federal estate tax upon death. Generally, the full amount of the retirement plan is taxed in the participant's estate for federal estate tax purposes. If, however, the participant's surviving spouse is the beneficiary, it is possible that there will be no estate taxes due to the unlimited marital deduction.

PENNSYLVANIA INHERITANCE TAX

Qualified retirement plans and IRAs are exempt from Pennsylvania inheritance tax to the extent that the participant did not have the right to possess, enjoy or assign the IRAs or retirement plans before death. The basic rule is that if the participant dies before reaching age $59^1/_2$, there will be no Pennsylvania inheritance tax due on their retirement plans or IRAs. (*See Chapter 7 for a more detailed discussion concerning the inheritance tax treatment of retirement plans.*)

Estate Planning for Retirement Plan Distributions During Lifetime

If the participant can afford it, he should consider deferring distributions from his IRA or retirement plan.

A key word regarding estate planning for retirement plan distributions is deferral. If the participant can afford it, he should consider deferring distributions from his IRA or retirement plan as long as possible. This deferral will permit the continued growth of the plan on a tax-deferred basis. The law requires that certain minimum distributions be taken from the plan. The reason for this policy is that these plans have been established to be retirement plans and not wealth building plans. These minimum distribution rules are intended to force funds out of the plan and expose the required distributions to income tax.

MINIMUM DISTRIBUTION RULES

Annual minimum distributions to the plan participant are required to begin on or before the participant's required beginning date (RBD). (Keep in mind: The RBD is April 1 of the year following the calendar year in which the participant reaches age 70½.) Once the participant has reached his required beginning date, the IRS rules establish the minimum annual distributions that must be taken by the plan participant. As of January 1, 2002, new regulations that significantly simplified the rules relating to retirement plan and IRA minimum distribution requirements took effect.

The minimum distribution required from your plan or traditional IRA is calculated in two steps:

Step One: Determine the total value of the investments in all your retirement plan accounts as of the last day of last year.

Step Two: Find your age as of the end of this year on the Uniform Table and divide the total value of your investments by the "applicable divisor" listed by your age.

> Consider the case of Mrs. Johnson, whose husband died last year. She is alone, owns her home, and has enough income to live on. Since she will be 72 at the end of this year and has $100,000 in her only IRA, as valued at the end of last year, she must receive a minimum of $4,098.36 during this year to avoid the 50% penalty ($100,000 divided by 24.4). Since she is spending a lot of time alone, but is in good health, her friends have been bugging her to get away and travel to the Holy Lands, which she has always wanted to do. Mrs. Johnson decides to spend her required distributions on a Mediteranean cruise throught the Middle East, instead of allowing the government to take half of this potential income in taxes.

The Uniform Table for Determining the Applicable Divisor

Age	Applicable Divisor	Age	Applicable Divisor
70	26.2	93	8.8
71	25.3	94	8.3
72	24.4	95	7.8
73	23.5	96	7.3
74	22.7	97	6.9
75	21.8	98	6.5
76	20.9	99	6.1
77	20.1	100	5.7
78	19.2	101	5.3
79	18.4	102	5.0
80	17.6	103	4.7
81	16.8	104	4.4
82	16.0	105	4.1
83	15.3	106	3.8
84	14.5	107	3.6
85	13.8	108	3.3
86	13.1	109	3.1
87	12.4	110	2.8
88	11.8	111	2.6
89	11.1	112	2.4
90	10.5	113	2.2
91	9.9	114	2.0
92	9.4	115 and older	1.8

Contrary to the old rules, the beneficiary of your IRA can now be changed after your required beginning date without having any effect upon the required distribution. Also, unlike the previous law, the distribution amount is not based upon who you name as the beneficiary of your account after your death. The minimum required distribution is calculated the same way whether you name a charity, a family member, an older parent or younger child as your beneficiary. The only exception to this rule is if you are (1) married to a person who is more than ten years younger than you, and (2) your spouse is the only beneficiary of your IRA. If that is your situation, the required distributions are based on the actual joint life expectancy of you and your younger spouse, and are lower than the Uniform Table.

DESIGNATED BENEFICIARIES

The designated beneficiary of a retirement plan or IRA must be an individual to achieve certain tax benefits. Since the participant's estate or charity is not an individual, the IRS does not consider either one to be a designated beneficiary. In addition to naming one individual, an acceptable beneficiary could be a group of individuals. For example, "all my children." When a group of individuals is named, the life expectancy of the oldest member of the group is used to calculate the required minimum distribution. In addition, all members in the group must be individuals. (Under certain limited circumstances, a trust may be named a beneficiary and the trust beneficiaries will be treated as designated beneficiaries if every trust beneficiary is an individual.)

The designated beneficiary of a retirement plan or IRA must be an individual to achieve certain tax benefits.

The designated beneficiary does not have to be finally determined until December 31 of the year following the participant's death. This permits many planning opportunities. Therefore, once a participant has died, it is important to engage the services of an experienced estate planner before making any distributions from the plan or IRA. (*See page 113.*)

SPOUSE AS DESIGNATED BENEFICIARY

There are a number of benefits to naming your spouse the beneficiary of your retirement plan or IRA. One benefit is that (regardless of whether you die before or after your RBD) if the sole beneficiary of your

IRA is your spouse, she has the option to roll over your benefit into her own IRA.*

If you die before your RBD, your spouse, if she does not roll over your IRA into her own, must take required distributions over his or her life expectancy. The payments must begin the later of the year you would have reached $70^1/_2$ or the year in which you died. If your spouse is older than you, she may wait until you would have reached age $70^1/_2$ and then roll over your IRA into her own IRA. This would allow her to defer the commencement of payment of the benefit for as long as possible.

If your spouse is named as beneficiary of your IRA or retirement plan, she will have the option to roll over the benefit into her own IRA.

If your spouse is the sole beneficiary and you die after your RBD, she may treat your IRA as her own if she does not roll over your IRA. Whether your spouse treats your IRA as her own or rolls it over into a new spousal IRA, she is permitted to have the IRA benefits paid out based on her age.

Another benefit to naming your spouse the beneficiary of your IRA is that if your spouse is more than ten years younger than you, the distribution period will be longer and, therefore, the required minimum distributions will be less than would be required for a non-spouse beneficiary.

Estate Planning for Retirement Plan Distributions after Death

In computing the required distributions to the beneficiaries of retirement plans after the death of the participant, the first consideration is the age at which the participant has died. If the participant dies before his RBD, then one set of rules apply. If the participant dies after his RBD, another set of rules apply (*see below*).

IF PARTICIPANT DIES BEFORE THE REQUIRED BEGINNING DATE

If the participant dies before his RBD, a non-spouse beneficiary must take required distributions over his or her life expectancy. If there

* Throughout this book either "he" or "she" may apply, even when only one pronoun is used.

are multiple beneficiaries who are all individuals, the distributions must be taken over the life expectancy of the oldest individual.

If the participant dies before his RBD and there is no designated beneficiary, then benefits must be distributed to the non-individual beneficiary no later than December 31 of the year that contains the fifth anniversary of the participant's death.

IF PARTICIPANT DIES AFTER THE REQUIRED BEGINNING DATE

If a participant dies after his RBD, remaining plan benefits or IRAs must be paid to the beneficiaries over the beneficiary's life expectancy. This is the same rule that applies if the participant dies *before* reaching his RBD. If there are multiple beneficiaries and the plan is not divided into separate accounts, distributions must be made over the life expectancy of the oldest individual beneficiary.

For purposes of calculating the required minimum distribution, the designated beneficiary is determined on December 31 of the year following the year of the participant's death (the DETERMINATION DATE). Thus, there is time allowed to formulate a strategy to create the longest possible payout. This could be done using disclaimers, for example.

If there is no designated beneficiary as of the determination date, the distribution period is the life expectancy of the participant determined in the year of his or her death reduced by one year for each year thereafter.

Estate Planning Considerations When Naming Retirement Plan Beneficiaries

NAMING A TRUST AS BENEFICIARY

A trust is not an individual and, therefore, does not qualify for the *tax benefits* reserved for designated beneficiaries who are individuals. In limited circumstances, nevertheless, IRS regulations will allow a trust the same benefits reserved for individuals as designated beneficiaries.

The concept is that the IRS will "look through" the trust and identify the individual beneficiaries of the trust as though they were individual beneficiaries of the IRA or retirement plan for purposes of calculating the minimum distribution amount. In order for a trust to qualify for such favorable treatment, it must satisfy four requirements:

The IRS may "look through" a trust and identify the individual beneficiaries of the trust as individual beneficiaries of the IRA or retirement plan for purposes of calculating the minimum distribution.

1. The trust must be valid under state law.
2. The trust beneficiaries must be individuals identifiable from the trust document. (This is necessary because the age of the oldest beneficiary is used to calculate the required minimum distribution amount.)
3. The trust must be irrevocable or become so after the participant's death.
4. A copy of the trust documentation must be given to the plan administrator.

These requirements must be satisfied no later than December 31 of the year following the year in which the participant dies. The only exception to this rule is if the spouse is the sole designated beneficiary of the trust and the spouse is more than ten years younger than the participant, then these requirements must be in place at the participant's RBD.

Even if there is only one trust beneficiary that is not an individual (for example a charity), the entire trust will be treated as having no individual named as a designated beneficiary. As a result, trust assets will be required to be paid out over the life expectancy of the participant and not that of any individual beneficiaries of the trust. If the participant dies before his RBD, benefits must be distributed no later than December 31 of the year that contains the fifth anniversary of the participant's death.

This negative result may be eliminated by having "non-individual" beneficiaries cash out or disclaim their interest in the trust or placing their interest into separate accounts before December 31 of the year following the year of the participant's death.

In addition, the trust must state that it is not to use any IRA distributions to pay debts or expenses of the participant's estate, including federal and state taxes. Without such language in the trust, the participant may be treated as not having a designated beneficiary since the participant's estate will be treated as a beneficiary of the retirement plan or IRA.

Q-TIP Trust as Beneficiary

Many IRA and qualified retirement plan participants desire to provide for their surviving spouse for life, continue the income tax deferral on the plan for as long as possible, and at the same time maintain control over the ultimate disposition of the remaining benefits at the surviving spouse's death. In addition, they may desire to qualify their retirement plans for the unlimited marital deduction from the federal estate tax. To achieve these multiple goals, the participant must name a trust the beneficiary of his plan or IRA.

> Only the Q-TIP trust qualifies for the marital deduction from estate tax at the participant's death, and at the same time enables the participant to control his trust assets after the death of his surviving spouse.

If the participant dies before age 70½ and the surviving spouse is the sole designated beneficiary of the plan or IRA, payments do not have to begin to be made to the surviving spouse until the participant would have reached age 70½. If a Q-TIP trust is used, however, the ultimate beneficiaries of the Q-TIP trust are treated as the designated beneficiaries of the plan or IRA. If amounts are permitted to be accumulated in the Q-TIP trust for the benefit of the ultimate beneficiaries, the rule permitting the surviving spouse to postpone distributions until the participant would have reached age 70½ is not available. The result is that distributions from the plan or IRA must begin in the year immediately following the year of the participant's death.

This result can be avoided if the Q-TIP trust requires that distributions to the surviving spouse be made in an amount that is the greater of either the income earned by the assets in the retirement plan or IRA, or the required minimum distributions based on the surviving spouse's age. In this case, no amounts distributed from the retirement plan are accumulated in the trust for the benefit of the ultimate beneficiaries.

Therefore, the surviving spouse would be permitted to delay taking his required minimum distributions until he reaches age $70^1/_2$.

CREDIT SHELTER TRUST AS BENEFICIARY

It may not be advisable to name a credit shelter trust the beneficiary of a retirement plan or IRA.

It may not be advisable to name a credit shelter trust the beneficiary of a retirement plan or IRA. One disadvantage is that naming the trust the beneficiary (instead of the spouse) prevents the surviving spouse from rolling over the funds into her own IRA. Another disadvantage to using IRAs to fund the credit shelter trust is that the IRA's distributions may be subject to income tax when received by the trust, and the trust's income tax rate might be higher than the surviving spouse's. In addition, if the trust pays the taxes, it reduces the amount that will pass free of federal estate tax from the credit shelter trust upon the death of the surviving spouse. There are cases, however, when a substantial portion of a participant's estate is made up of plan benefits and IRAs and there are no other assets available to fund the credit shelter trust.

There are two basic strategies to using retirement plans or IRAs to fund the credit shelter trust of the first spouse to die:

1. First, the participant could designate the credit shelter trust the beneficiary of the participant's IRAs to the extent necessary to fund the credit shelter trust.
2. A second option is to name the spouse the primary beneficiary and the credit shelter trust the CONTINGENT BENEFICIARY.

Using the second approach, if the participant dies before his spouse, the surviving spouse has the option to disclaim the exact value of IRAs needed to fully fund the participant's credit shelter trust. The remaining portion of the IRA not disclaimed could be rolled over into the surviving spouse's IRA. This option is preferred due to its flexibility. If the estate tax is repealed, or if the participant has other available assets, the surviving spouse can simply roll over the deceased spouse's IRA into her own IRA. In addition, the use of the disclaimer strategy enables the surviving spouse to compare the benefit of tax-deferred income with the benefit of estate tax savings at the time of the participant's death. To maintain the option to disclaim, the designation of the spouse should remain revocable during the life of the participant.

Revocable Living Trust as Beneficiary

Revocable living trusts often contain credit shelter trusts and Q-TIP trusts within them. The same rules regarding credit shelter trusts and Q-TIP trusts apply when naming a revocable living trust as beneficiary.

Charitable Remainder Trusts

A CHARITABLE REMAINDER TRUST can be named the beneficiary of an IRA. This is an option for those who wish to provide an income stream for a surviving spouse, yet also make a charitable contribution. One drawback to naming a charitable remainder trust the beneficiary of an IRA is that distributions can only be made to the surviving spouse in a *fixed dollar amount* or a *fixed percentage rate.* This means that the use of the charitable remainder trust eliminates the ability of the trustee to make additional distributions of principal to the surviving spouse for her needs.

The charitable remainder trust eliminates the ability of the trustee to make additional distributions to the surviving spouse for her needs.

Upon the death of the surviving spouse, the trust terminates and the assets remaining are paid to one or more qualified charities. If the surviving spouse is the only non-charitable beneficiary, then the entire value of the IRA passing to the charitable remainder trust would be deductible for federal estate tax purposes when the participant dies. The surviving spouse's interest would qualify for the unlimited marital deduction and the value of the trust assets going to charity qualifies for the charitable deduction. There is no federal income tax due when the IRA is paid to the trust upon the death of the participant because the charitable remainder trust is tax exempt. The surviving spouse will pay income tax on the amount that she receives from the trust each year.

Another beneficial strategy utilizing charitable remainder trusts occurs when the participant establishes a charitable remainder trust and names his children the income beneficiaries. The charitable remainder trust would then be designated as the *contingent* beneficiary of the participant's retirement plan or IRA. The result is that during lifetime, both the participant and his spouse have full lifetime rights to the plan assets. After the death of both the participant and his spouse, the undistributed assets in the retirement plan or IRA will pass to the charitable remainder trust in a lump sum and provide income to his children for their lifetimes. Since the charitable remainder trust pays no income tax, the transfer of retirement plan benefits into the charitable remainder trust is tax free.

Transfer of retirement plan benefits into the charitable remainder trust is tax free.

The benefit of this plan is that the children receive the income from the full value of the retirement plan or IRA assets because those assets are not reduced by income tax. In addition, the client's estate receives an estate tax charitable deduction for the present value of the remainder interest that will go to charity upon the death of the children. Using this plan, the children may receive more from the charitable remainder trust during their lifetimes than they would have received from the qualified plan. In terms of wealth replacement, since the charitable remainder trust does not pay out to charity until the death of the participant's children, the wealth replacement is not necessary until the children's death and not the participant's death. The wealth replacement insurance will be less because of the insuring of a younger generation.

CHARITY AS BENEFICIARY

Naming a qualified charity the beneficiary of a retirement plan or IRA may be advisable since charities are exempt from income tax.

Since a charity is not an individual, if the charity is only one of a number of beneficiaries of a retirement plan or IRA, the participant will be treated as not having any individuals named as a designated beneficiary. This will cause a higher minimum required distribution after his death because only the participant's life expectancy will apply when calculating the payout period for the distribution of plan assets. Also, if the participant dies before his RBD, the retirement plan or IRA will be treated as having no designated beneficiary and the five-year rule will apply. (*See page 112.*) By specifying that the charitable organization is entitled to a separate account of the IRA this result can be avoided. Therefore, when naming a charity as a beneficiary of a retirement plan or IRA, it is important to specify the specific portion or account that goes to the charity.

Many people with charitable intent have accumulated large IRAs. The amount given to charity can be enhanced by giving the portion of their estate made up of retirement plans or IRAs to charity. This amount will not be subject to income tax when distributed to the charity and, in addition, will be a deduction from the federal estate tax.

Mr. Garcia had an estate comprised of $50,000 cash and an IRA valued at $50,000, for a total of $100,000. He wanted to leave $50,000 to his college because he felt that his education had made him successful throughout his life. He wished to divide the remainder of his estate equally between his two children. Mr. Garcia went to his attorney and told him that he wanted to pass the $50,000 in cash to his alma mater. This would allow his children to share the $50,000 IRA. Fortunately, he had a knowledgeable attorney who had a much better plan.

His attorney explained that if the cash went to the college and the IRA to the children, the children would have to pay income tax as they received the IRA distributions. On the other hand, if the college was named the designated beneficiary of the IRA, the college, a nonprofit educational organization (a charity), would receive the $50,000 from the IRA tax free.

Summary

Many people forget to consider their retirement plans and IRAs when doing estate planning. The importance of coordinating the beneficiary designation on your retirement plans and IRAs with your estate plan cannot be overstated. In addition, with the number of taxes involved with retirement plan benefits, distribution during both lifetime and after death should be carefully considered.

Part IV

How Much Will Your Family Need To Pay in Taxes in the Event of Your Death?

"When you can't solve the problem, manage it."

– Robert H. Schuller

7

Understanding Pennsylvania's Inheritance Tax

Topics Include

Who Must Pay the Tax?

What Are the Tax Rates?

Calculating the Tax

Jointly-Owned Assets & the Inheritance Tax

Pennsylvania Inheritance Tax Planinng Strategies

Pennsylvania Estate Tax

Introduction

AS YOU WORK WITH YOUR TEAM to formulate your estate plan, you'll find the input of a qualified estate planning attorney and an accountant experienced in Pennsylvania's tax laws invaluable. Why? Because in no other area of estate planning for Pennsylvania residents is there more confusion than Pennsylvania's inheritance tax. Who will owe Pennsylvania's taxes on inherited property and assets, and how much will they owe? You'll want to have a clear understanding of the ins and outs of the inheritance tax, so that your estate plan is written to minimize taxes and maximize benefits to your beneficiaries.

The purpose of this chapter is to give you a solid understanding of the fundamentals of the Pennsylvania inheritance tax so that you can make appropriate arrangements in your estate now to minimize the impact of this tax on your estate in the future. Armed with the strategies about to be discussed, you will be able to take advantage of the tax saving strategies covered at the end of the chapter. This chapter also covers the PENNSYLVANIA ESTATE TAX and what happens to your safe deposit box upon your death. In addition, if you are named executor of someone else's estate, you will have a road map to follow regarding the calculation and payment of the Pennsylvania inheritance tax.

How significant is this tax? During the fiscal year ending June 30, 2001, the total inheritance and estate tax collected by the Pennsylvania Department of Revenue was close to $800,000,000.

Pennsylvania's Top Twenty Counties for 2000–2001 Total Inheritance & Estate Tax Collections

Rank	County	Total Collected
1	Allegheny	$104,300,000
2	Montgomery	$103,900,000
3	Philadelphia	$ 80,900,000
4	Delaware	$ 52,800,000
5	Chester	$ 48,100,000
6	Bucks	$ 36,700,000
7	Erie	$ 29,500,000
8	Lancaster	$ 24,800,000
9	Westmoreland	$ 21,400,000
10	Luzerne	$ 19,200,000
11	Berks	$ 17,500,000
12	York	$ 17,400,000
13	Lehigh	$ 16,800,000
14	Northampton	$ 15,700,000
15	Cumberland	$ 13,100,000
16	Dauphin	$ 12,900,000
17	Lackawanna	$ 12,600,000
18	Washington	$ 10,900,000
19	Butler	$ 8,900,000
20	Franklin	$ 8,500,000

Overview of the Tax

The personal representative of the estate has a duty to confirm that the taxes are paid on assets passing through the estate.

Simply put, Pennsylvania's inheritance tax is a tax on the privilege of receiving an inheritance. It's not a tax upon the assets transferred, nor is it a tax upon the persons receiving assets. The one who receives the assets, however, is ultimately responsible to pay the tax. The personal representative of the estate has a duty to *confirm* that the taxes are paid on assets passing through the estate. If there is a will, it usually specifies that the tax should be paid from estate assets as an expense of administration of the estate. This is not necessarily always the best plan for the payment of taxes. Therefore, a key issue of every estate plan that must be carefully considered is the answer to the question, "How will the inheritance tax be paid?" Since the tax is on the privilege of receiving assets, the key to understanding this tax is remembering that it is imposed upon transfers of assets. Transferred assets that incur the tax include:

- All real estate located in Pennsylvania. (Real estate located outside of Pennsylvania is not subject to the tax.)
- All tangible personal assets located in Pennsylvania (i.e., cash, automobiles, furniture, and antiques).
- All intangible assets such as stocks, bonds, bank accounts and other similar types of investments. (Intangible assets is taxed regardless of whether or not it is located in Pennsylvania.)

Who Must Pay the Tax?

The party responsible to pay the tax is the recipient of the inheritance. Although wills are usually written instructing the executor to use estate money to pay the tax before any distributions are made, those receiving an inheritance from jointly owned assets, annuities, transfer on death investment accounts, as well as those receiving assets through a will, are subject to the tax.

A unique aspect regarding the collection of the tax is the Pennsylvania law that permits mutual funds and other investment

The party responsible to pay the tax is the recipient of the inheritance.

accounts to be registered as transfer on death accounts. Upon the death of the owner of such an account, the mutual fund or investment company transfers the deceased owner's assets to the named beneficiary and provides written notice of the transfer to the department of revenue. The department of revenue then sends a billing notice to the recipient of the T.O.D. account requesting payment of the inheritance tax. This is the same procedure followed for joint bank accounts.

What Are the Tax Rates?

The tax rate imposed on taxable transfers depends on the relationship of your beneficiary to you. The following tax rates apply:*

Transfers to the following are tax free:

- A surviving spouse
- Charity
- Transfers from a deceased child age 21 years or younger to his or her parent or step-parent

Transfers to the following are taxed at the rate of 4.5%:

- Grandparents
- Parents
- Children and their spouses
- Grandchildren and their spouses
- Stepchildren and their spouses
- Adopted children and their spouses

Transfers to siblings are taxed at the rate of 12%: (A sibling is an individual who has at least one parent in common with the decedent whether by blood or adoption.)

Transfers to all others are taxed at the rate of 15%.

* Effective for the estates of those dying after June 30, 2000.

Transfers That Are Taxable for the Inheritance Tax

GENERAL RULE

All assets transferred to others upon your death are taxable *whether or not you have a will* (with some exceptions). This includes transfers from a revocable living trust. Although revocable living trusts have many benefits, they do not minimize the Pennsylvania inheritance tax.

Although revocable living trusts have many benefits, they do not minimize the Pennsylvania inheritance tax.

The transfer on death designation on mutual funds and investments, jointly owned assets and annuities all may avoid probate due to beneficiary designations, but these investments are still taxable for the inheritance tax.

JOINT ASSETS

Any assets jointly owned by you and others is subject to the tax, although only to the extent of your ownership. The taxable portion of jointly owned assets can be calculated by determining the fractional interest you own in the joint property and the value of that fractional interest will be taxed. An exception to this rule is that assets passing by right of survivorship to a surviving spouse are not taxed. The value of

Jointly-Owned Assets & Inheritance Tax

Father owned a hunting cabin in Bradford County jointly with his two brothers. The deed stated they owned the cabin as joint tenants with rights of survivorship. When Father died, Father's one-third interest in the hunting cabin was automatically transferred to his two brothers. To calculate the inheritance tax, only one-third of the value of the cabin would be taxed in Father's estate since Father only owned a one-third interest in it, and at his death that interest was transferred to his two brothers.

the fractional interest is determined by dividing the total value of the jointly owned asset by the total number of owners. This is different from the federal rule where the total value of joint assets owned by the decedent with a non-spouse are taxed in the decedent's estate unless the surviving owners can prove their contribution to the joint account.

CERTAIN LIFETIME TRANSFERS WILL BE TAXED AT DEATH

Gifts made within twelve months of death are taxed upon the donor's death if the value of the gift was greater than $3,000 to any one person in any calendar year. This rule causes confusion because of the federal gift tax annual exclusion of $11,000 per year. For example, if Grandpa makes a death-bed gift of $11,000 to his daughter, the entire $11,000 will be excluded from his estate for federal estate tax purposes if that was the only gift he gave her that year. Only $3,000 will be excluded from the Pennsylvania inheritance tax, however. The remaining $8,000 of the gift will be taxed for Pennsylvania inheritance tax purposes.

The One Year Look-Back Rule

Let's assume Mother names her daughter, Nancy, a joint owner on her checking account with $10,000 in it, and Mother passes away within twelve months. Mother has made a gift to Nancy because the $10,000 checking account had two joint owners. The one-half interest owned by Mother upon her death would be taxed to the extent of $5,000 (one half of $10,000). In addition, since Mother gave Nancy a $5,000 gift within one year of her death, only $3,000 will be excluded from the inheritance tax and, therefore, $2,000 will be taxed in Mother's estate as well as the $5,000 representing Mother's one-half interest in the joint account. If, on the other hand, Nancy dies before Mother, Mother would have to pay inheritance tax on the $5,000 value of joint assets that she would receive from Nancy.

(This one year look-back rule also applies for property and financial assets placed in joint names within one year of death.)

A second example of a transfer made during lifetime that results in tax at death is when the decedent transfers assets and keeps a lifetime interest in the transferred assets. An example of this would be a revocable living trust that a bamk manager, Roger, established during his lifetime. He re-registered all of his assets into the name of his living trust and reserved the right to all the income and control of the trust. Upon Roger's death, the full amount of his revocable living trust will be taxed for inheritance tax purposes, because he reserved the right to control the trust.

A third lifetime transfer that results in a tax at death is when the decedent transfers assets and reserves a life estate. For example, Mother and Father transfer the farm to their son, Elvin, but reserve the right to live in the farmhouse until their deaths. At that time, the fair market value of the farm will be taxed for inheritance tax purposes. This is a common tax trap that can be minimized with adequate planning. Caution should always be used when transferring assets and reserving a life estate.

Assets Not Subject to Pennsylvania Inheritance Tax

LIFE INSURANCE

The proceeds of life insurance are not taxable for the Pennsylvania inheritance tax.

The proceeds of life insurance are not taxable for the Pennsylvania inheritance tax. This exemption applies whether the proceeds are payable to a named beneficiary or to your estate.

Even though life insurance proceeds payable to your estate are not subject to Pennsylvania inheritance tax, it is still important to have insurance proceeds paid directly to an individual or trust as the beneficiary. Failure to name a beneficiary on your life insurance policy results in the death benefit being paid to your probate estate, which exposes the proceeds to creditors of the estate and increases estate administration expenses.

RETIREMENT PLAN BENEFITS

The general rule is that Pennsylvania will tax your retirement plan benefits if you are age $59^1/_2$ or older when you pass away. If you are under $59^1/_2$ and a withdrawal from your IRA or qualified retirement plan would incur a 10% penalty for early withdrawl, your IRA or qualified retirement plan is not subject to Pennsylvania inheritance tax. You should review your plan carefully to determine whether the benefits are taxable.

SURVIVORSHIP ASSETS OWNED BY HUSBAND & WIFE

Assets that are owned jointly by husband and wife are exempt from the tax when the first spouse dies.

Assets that are owned jointly by husband and wife is exempt from the tax when the first spouse dies. All other assets passing to a surviving spouse at the death of the first spouse are not exempt from the tax, but are taxed at a rate of 0%. An inheritance tax return must be filed with the department of revenue reporting non-joint assets passing to a surviving spouse, even though it is taxed at 0%. If, for example, the first spouse to pass away had an automobile registered solely in their name, an inheritance tax return would be required, although the return would show no tax due. If all assets was jointly owned by spouses, then at the time the first passed away, no inheritance tax return would even be required to be filed.

Valuation

Since the inheritance tax is based upon the value of your assets on your date of death, valuation issues are very important. The value of the assets transferred is its "fair market value." The determination of the fair market value must be reported to the department of revenue on the tax return. Therefore, letters from banks and stock brokerage firms and insurance companies confirming the exact value of assets on the date of death need to be requested immediately. The value of real

The value of assets transferred is its "fair market value."

estate should be determined by requesting an appraisal from a qualified real estate appraiser who will provide the fair market value of the real estate on the date of death of the owner. If the real estate is sold within a reasonable period of time following the date of death, the sale price is generally accepted as the fair market value and an appraisal would not be necessary.

Deductions

There are a number of expenses which may be deducted from the total value of all taxable assets transferred. These deductions will lower the inheritance tax.

ADMINISTRATIVE EXPENSES

Administrative expenses include accounting and legal expenses. Funeral and burial expenses and the cost of a family burial lot are also deductible to the extent that they are reasonable and customary. Reasonable expenses for the purchase and erection of a monument or gravestone on the decedent's burial lot are also deductible. Expenses relating to the performance of religious rites or services or ceremonies are deductible as well.

LIABILITIES OF THE DECEDENT

Unpaid liabilities and debts incurred by the decedent before death are deductible. This includes checks written by the decedent prior to death that were outstanding as of the date of death.

FAMILY EXEMPTION

The family exemption of $3,500 is also deductible for purposes of the Pennsylvania inheritance tax. This family exemption amount is given to the surviving spouse if he or she resided with the decedent. If a decedent did not have a surviving spouse, then any child who was a member of the same household of the decedent, may claim the family exemption. If there is no spouse or child, the exemption may be claimed by a parent so long as they were members of the same household as the decedent.

The family exemption is allowable only against assets which pass by a will or by intestacy and must be payable from the probate estate of the decedent. It may not be claimed as a deduction if there are not sufficient probate assets to satisfy the exemption.

How To Calculate the Tax

The Pennsylvania inheritance tax is calculated by multiplying the relevant percentage times the value of the assets transferred to each beneficiary. For example, Grandmother's will stated that one-half of her estate goes to Grandfather, one-fourth to her son and the remaining one-fourth to her niece. If the estate is $100,000, then Grandfather's $50,000 would be taxed at 0%, son's $25,000 would be taxed at 4.5% and niece's $25,000 would be taxed at 15%.

Returns & Payment of Tax

The personal representative is required to file the inheritance tax return and pay the tax.

The personal representative (the executor if there is a will or the administrator if there is no will) of the estate is required to file the inheritance tax return and pay the tax. The general practice is that the personal representative will pay the tax using assets in the estate before making any distributions from the estate to the beneficiaries. The tax is due within nine months of the date of death and the inheritance tax return is filed at the register of wills office of the county in which the decedent was a resident. There is a discount of 5% of the amount of inheritance tax actually paid, if it is paid within three months of the date of death. The return itself is not required to be filed within the three-month deadline, but any taxes paid by that time qualify for the discount.

Anyone receiving assets as a joint survivor, or as a recipient of transfer on death assets, is required to file a return and pay any tax due on their inheritance if the tax is not paid by the personal representative. In rare situations when the personal representative does not have enough money in the estate to pay the tax, the personal representative

Anyone who knowingly fails to file a return, will be personally liable for a penalty.

will contact the beneficiaries and request them to contribute money to the estate, which can be used to pay the tax. Anyone who knowingly fails to file a return will be personally liable for a penalty of 25% of the tax due or $1,000 whichever is less.

Inheritance tax return forms may be obtained at the register of wills office in any county courthouse or at any of the Pennsylvania Department of Revenue District offices. These offices can be located by referring to the government pages in your phone book.

Pennsylvania Inheritance Tax Planning Strategies

Although inheritance tax rates are relatively low, there are strategies to reduce it even more.

TRUSTS FOR THE SOLE USE OF SURVIVING SPOUSES

When a decedent's will or living trust establishes a trust for their surviving spouse (spousal trust), under certain circumstances the spousal trust may have inheritance tax benefits.

A common situation that raises this issue is when there is a credit shelter trust in the will of the first spouse to die. If the credit shelter trust provisions make income and/or principal available for the SOLE USE of the surviving spouse, no tax is due at the first spouse's death, but the tax shall then be due upon the death of the surviving spouse. If, however, the credit shelter trust permits the trustee to make distributions to anyone other than the surviving spouse during her lifetime (her children for example), then the inheritance tax must be paid upon the death of the first spouse. Credit shelter trusts should be carefully worded. If there is no reason to provide for the children during the surviving spouse's lifetime (if all children are adults, for example), then distributions to children should not be permitted by the credit shelter trust. This will keep open the option of being able to wait and not pay the tax until the death of the surviving spouse.

> Consider the case of James and Deborah: James died and left a trust for Deborah, his surviving spouse. The trust is to pay her income during her lifetime and, at Deborah's death, the remainder is to go to their three children. As long as Deborah is the only one to receive any interest in the trust during her lifetime, there is no inheritance tax due upon James' death. Upon Deborah's subsequent death, however, the value of the trust assets that are transferred to the children will be fully taxed based on the value of the trust assets at the time of their mother's death.
>
> The personal representative (Deborah or whomever James named) may, however, elect to pay the tax upon James' death. If this is the case, then no tax will be due when Deborah passes away.

If the personal representative elects to pay the tax upon the death of the first spouse, only the value of that portion of the trust passing to the children upon the death of the surviving spouse will be taxed. In other words, there is a calculation made to arrive at the value of the trust that belongs to the surviving spouse — known as his LIFE ESTATE. There is, however, a tax upon the value of the trust that ultimately goes to the children. This will always be less than the full value of the trust at the first spouse's death and is know as the remainder. The tax, upon the death of the first spouse, is based on the value or the remainder. The value of the life estate is subtracted from the total value of the trust to determine the value of the remainder. Only the remainder value is taxed when the personal representative pays the tax at the first spouse's death. If the personal representative pays no tax upon the death of the first spouse, then the tax on the transfer from the trust to the children at the death of the surviving spouse will be based on the total value of the trust at that time, which may be greater than the remainder value.

What factors should be considered in deciding whether to pay the tax on a sole use trust upon the participant's death or upon the death of the surviving spouse? First, let's consider situations where the personal representative should consider *not* paying the tax until after the death of the surviving spouse:

1. If the surviving spouse cannot afford any reduction in income and will have a need for every dollar in the credit shelter trust, it may be better to not pay the tax until after the death of the surviving spouse.
2. If the surviving spouse plans to move out of state, the personal representative should consider not paying the tax at the first death.

When would it be advisable to pay the tax when the participant dies? If the trust is funded with exempt assets such as life insurance or foreign real estate, electing to pay tax upon the first spouse's death may not incur any Pennsylvania inheritance tax.

An Example of the Tax Treatment of a Trust for the Sole Use of a Spouse

Careful planning must precede decisions about the timing of the inheritance tax. This example illustrates a procedure that should always be engaged when tax planing for a sole use trust:

Keith, a conscientious husband and careful planner, preceded his wife in death. Prior to his passing away, he placed $100,000 in a trust for the sole use of his wife, Millie. After Millie's death, what remains in the trust will be distributed to their children. Millie was sixty-five at the time Keith died. Assuming an IRS rate of 6%, the value of Millie's life interest is $58,291 and the value of the children's remainder interest is $41,709 (what they will receive at Millie's death). Assume further that Millie lives her normal life expectancy (to age eighty-five) and the value of the trust grows at the rate of 4% per year to $219,112 at the time Millie dies. The tax due at Keith's death, if the executor makes the election to pay tax then, would be $1,877 ($41,709 x 4.5%). If, on the other hand, the family waits to pay the inheritance tax when Millie dies, the tax due would be $9,860 ($219,112 x 4.5%), assuming the tax rate is the same.

TAX PLANNING STRATEGIES USING LIFE INSURANCE

Since there is no inheritance tax on life insurance, a tax strategy is to give a beneficiary life insurance instead of cash bequests if the beneficiary is subject to Pennsylvania inheritance tax at the 12% or 15% rate.

An Example of Strategic Planning with Life Insurance

Barney had a $100,000 life insurance policy payable to his children, and his will gives a cash bequest of $100,000 to a friend. There is a 15% inheritance tax on the $100,000 going to his friend. If, instead, he names his friend the beneficiary of the life insurance (which is not subject to Pennsylvania inheritance tax) and his will leaves the $100,000 to his children, the total Pennsylvania inheritance tax will be reduced by $10,500. This amount equals the difference between $100,000 taxed at 15% if the gift of cash goes to his friend under his will ($15,000.00) compared to $100,000 taxed at 4.5% ($4,500.00) if the gift of cash goes instead to his children under his will.

Another inheritance tax planning strategy using life insurance is to name a trust the beneficiary of life insurance to be held for the benefit of your spouse. By naming the trust beneficiary, the life insurance keeps its tax-free status even after the death of the surviving spouse. For example, assume life insurance proceeds are payable to a credit shelter trust for the sole use of a spouse. In this case, the executor should make the election to have the trust taxed at the death of the first spouse. The result is that the full amount of insurance proceeds will be taxed at 0% at the death of the first spouse and no tax will be due at the death of the surviving spouse.

SPECIAL VALUATION AVAILABLE FOR FARMLAND

Real estate is usually valued at its highest and best use for purposes of calculating Pennsylvania inheritance tax. Land devoted to

Real estate is usually valued at its highest and best use for purposes of calculating Pennsylvania inheritance tax.

"agricultural use," "agricultural reserve" or "forest reserve," however, is eligible for a lower value based on its *actual* use as opposed to its *highest and best possible* use. In those areas of Pennsylvania where farmland is in areas of rapid development, this special valuation can result in a significant reduction in the inheritance tax. To qualify as agricultural use for inheritance tax purposes, the land must have been so used for at least three years preceding death and be no less than ten acres in area or have an anticipated yearly income of $2,000. Agricultural reserve or forest reserve land must be no less than ten acres.

If the use of any land valued lower than market value based on its actual use is changed within seven years of the decedent's death, and the land is no longer used in either agriculture or forest reserve, the owner at the time the use of the land is changed is liable for back taxes plus interest from the date of death. The tax due is equal to the difference between the taxes paid on the preferred value and the taxes which would have been paid based on the land's market value on the date of death of the decedent, plus interest. The owner of land that is preferentially valued is required to notify the register of wills office of the county in which the land is located in the event of any change in the use of the land.

Gifts can be made not only by cash or check, but also by re-titling property or financial assets into joint names. Mary had always been very close to her son, Steve, who had lived and worked in his hometown to remain close to her. Several years after Mary lost her husband, she decided that she would put her house into joint ownership in her and Steve's name. Since the house was worth $100,000, she made a gift to him of one half the value of her home, $50,000. Twelve years later when Mary passed away, Steve's tax liability was reduced from 4.5% of $100,000 to 4.5% of $50,000, because only one half of the value of the home was transferred to Steve upon her death.

Many counties in Pennsylvania have enacted the preferential real estate tax assessment procedures under the Pennsylvania Farmland and Forest Land Assessment Act of 1974. This is commonly known as Act 319 or Clean and Green. If land is assessed by the county under the provisions of Act 319, the valuation determined by the county tax assessor for Act 319 purposes may be accepted by the department of revenue as its value as agricultural use for inheritance tax purposes.

LIFETIME GIFTS REDUCE THE PENNSYLVANIA INHERITANCE TAX

Because Pennsylvania has no gift tax, there are planning opportunities available by making gifts during one's lifetime. Except with regard to gifts greater than $3,000 made within one year of death, gifted assets are not subject to inheritance tax. Lifetime gifts can be especially beneficial if you are leaving your estate to beneficiaries taxed at the 15% rate (nephews and nieces or friends). You will save 15¢ in taxes on every dollar gifted and also remove from your estate future appreciation on the transferred assets as well as the future income generated by such assets after the transfer.

Gifts of joint ownership carry a number of risks.

Gifts of joint ownership carry a number of risks, however. In the previous example, if Steve had died first, Mother would have had to pay inheritance tax of 4.5% on $50,000 at his death for the privilege of receiving her own property back (except when the son is 21 years of age or younger, when there would be no tax). To add insult to injury, another tax of 4.5% of the full value of the home would be due at Mother's death because she would once again own the entire house. Also, because the son has an ownership interest, if he is married and gets a divorce, a portion of his interest may be considered a marital asset subject to equitable distribution.

Another risk of joint ownership of assets with a non-spouse is that the son's interest would be subject to his creditors. Lastly, family conflict regarding other children might result if assets are placed into joint ownership with only one child.

When making lifetime gifts, it is important to consider that removal of an asset from your estate by lifetime gift prevents the asset from receiving a STEPPED-UP BASIS for income tax purposes upon your death. Therefore, with the maximum CAPITAL GAINS TAX rate in 2002 at

20%, gifting an appreciated asset during lifetime may not be as beneficial as simply holding onto the asset until death and paying the Pennsylvania inheritance tax which is only 4.5% to children. This assumes there are no federal estate taxes to be saved by gifting.

> Assume Mother owns stock with a value of $100,000, which cost Mother $10,000. If Mother gifted the stock to her daughter Lisa, and Lisa then sold the stock, Lisa would have to pay a capital gains tax of $18,000 ($100,000 minus the mother's cost of $10,000 is $90,000, on which the 20% capital gains tax would be $18,000). If, on the other hand, Mother retained the stock until her death, the receipt of the stock by Lisa would have been subject to inheritance tax of $4,500. When Lisa sold the stock, however, there would have been no capital gains tax because the basis for the stock would be "stepped up" to the value at Mother's death. This would result in a tax savings of $13,500.

Pennsylvania Estate Tax

In addition to the inheritance tax, Pennsylvania also imposes an estate tax that is payable only if there is federal estate tax due. The federal estate tax provides a state death tax credit for the amount of Pennsylvania inheritance tax that is actually paid to Pennsylvania. In unusual circumstances, this federal estate tax credit can be an amount greater than the amount of Pennsylvania inheritance tax actually paid. When this occurs, the Pennsylvania estate tax is required to be paid. The amount of Pennsylvania estate tax due is equal to the amount of the federal credit for state death taxes permitted as a credit to lower the federal estate tax minus the amount of Pennsylvania inheritance tax actually paid. This tax is due within nine months after death and a copy of the federal estate tax return is due with payment along with a statement of the manner of the calculation of the tax.

It should be noted that under the Taxpayer Relief Act of 2001, this state death tax credit is being phased out. In its place will be the allowance of inheritance tax paid as a deduction from the federal estate tax.

> The Pennsylvania Department of Revenue receives about 60,000 inheritance tax returns each year. Of those returns, only about 2,000 to 3,000 are required to file Pennsylvania estate tax returns. In the next few years it is estimated that Pennsylvania's estate tax collections will range from $40,000,000 to $70,000,000. Pennsylvania estate tax collections will decrease, however, as the federal estate tax lifetime exemption amount increases over the next few years. In addition, the federal estate tax credit for state death taxes paid is scheduled to be phased out. Since this credit for state death taxes is the source of Pennsylvania's estate tax collections, the result of its phase-out is an eventual phase-out of the Pennsylvania estate tax as well.

Limitations on Entry into Decedent's Safe Deposit Box

When someone dies, there are restrictions on entry into their safe deposit box if it was in their name alone (or in their name and one or more other persons not their spouse). The rule is that no person having knowledge of the death of a decedent is permitted to enter the decedent's safe deposit box. There are limited exceptions to this rule. Entry is permitted under these circumstances:

- To remove the will and cemetery deed,
- In the presence of a bank employee who makes a record of the contents,

- In the presence of a representative of the department of revenue who makes an inventory of the contents, or
- Under a court order.

Any individual who enters a safe deposit box having knowledge of the death of the owner is guilty of a misdemeanor subject to a fine not exceeding $10,000 or imprisonment not exceeding one year.

Summary

Pennsylvania's inheritance tax is not a complex tax, but it is difficult to minimize. There are, however, a number of fundamental strategies that you should consider to plan for the possible effects of the Pennsylvania inheritance tax upon your heirs. With a maximum tax rate of 15%, this tax should not be taken lightly.

8

The Federal Estate & Gift Taxes Explained

Topics Include

Who Must Pay the Federal Estate Tax

Estate Tax Rates

Estate Tax Deductions & Credits

An Overview of the Gift Tax

Income Tax Problems Related to the Gift Tax

The Generation-Skipping Transfer Tax

Introduction

ONE REASON IT IS IMPORTANT TO HAVE A COMPETENT TEAM of professionals assisting you with your estate plan is the fact that not only do laws frequently change, but they can change and then revert back! This is the case with the Tax Relief Act of

2001. In this chapter we will review the important implications of this "Now You See It, Now You Don't" tax law.

On June 7, 2001, President Bush signed into law THE ECONOMIC GROWTH AND TAX RELIEF RECONCILIATION ACT OF 2001, known as the TAX RELIEF ACT OF 2001. This law significantly revised the federal estate and gift tax laws. The new law increased the amount that can be left to heirs free of estate tax to $1,000,000 for the years 2002 and 2003, with a graduated exemption scale reaching $3,500,000 for estate tax purposes in 2009. This LIFETIME EXCLUSION AMOUNT limits the number of people who need to plan for the tax. According to IRS figures, in 1999, only about 50,000 estates were subject to the federal estate tax. Of those estates, about 19,000 were valued at less than $1,000,000. The result is that only 30,000 estates would now be exposed to the federal estate tax, if estate sizes remained constant from 1999 to 2002.

The Tax Relief Act of 2001 expires on Dec 31, 2010.

There is an interesting "sunset" provision contained in this law, however, that makes the entire law expire on *December 31, 2010.* Of course, new legislation could extend the repeal date, but unless a new law is enacted by December 31, 2010, the estate and gift tax law will revert to that which was in existence prior to the Tax Relief Act of 2001. This factor is why some have dubbed this law the "Now You See It, Now You Don't" estate tax repeal. If estate taxes are a major concern, one should plan to stay alive until the year 2010 and pass away in that year! This chapter covers the highlights of this tax and how it is calculated.

Overview of the Federal Estate Tax

Before we can determine the amount of federal estate taxes due, we must first carefully inventory all the assets that are included in the decedent's GROSS ESTATE, then establish its value.

These steps must be taken because the federal estate tax is based upon the *fair market value* of assets owned by the decedent. This value is determined as of the date of the decedent's death (or six months later if the alternate valuation date is elected). Since the federal estate tax is imposed on the *transfer* of assets (not the assets themselves) it is known as a transfer tax. Unfortunately, it is also known as a death tax.

Who Must Pay the Tax?

The estate tax considers both the value of your assets and the year of your death to determine if any tax is due. Your estate must pay the tax only if its value on the date of your passing is greater than your lifetime exclusion amount (also known as APPLICABLE EXCLUSION AMOUNT, UNIFIED CREDIT AMOUNT and ESTATE TAX EXEMPTION). The table below shows the lifetime exclusion amounts established by the Tax Relief Act of 2001.

Lifetime Exclusions

Year of Death	Estate Tax Lifetime Exclusion	Unified Tax Credit	Gift Tax Lifetime Exclusion	Highest Estate & Gift Tax Rates
2002	$1 million	$345,800	$1 million	50%
2003	$1 million	$345,800	$1 million	49%
2004	$1.5 million	$555,800	$1 million	48%
2005	$1.5 million	$555,800	$1 million	47%
2006	$2 million	$780,800	$1 million	46%
2007	$2 million	$780,800	$1 million	45%
2008	$2 million	$780,800	$1 million	45%
2009	$3.5 million	$1,250,800	$1 million	45%
2010	Unlimited (Taxes Repealed)	—	$1 million	35% (Gift Tax Only)
2011 and after	$1 million	$345,800	$1 million	55%

What Are the Tax Rates?

Only estates with values greater than the lifetime exclusion amount are required to pay federal estate tax.

If your estate is valued at less than your lifetime exclusion amount, then no federal estate tax will be due upon your death. Only estates with values greater than the lifetime exclusion amount are required to pay federal estate tax.

The tax is calculated by first determining the tax due on the *entire estate* without considering your lifetime exclusion amount (*for a list of estate assets, see page 145*). The amount due on the entire estate is known as the gross tax due. Next, an amount known as the UNIFIED TAX CREDIT is subtracted from the gross tax due. The *net* amount represents the tax due for the estate. The unified tax credit reduces the estate tax liability dollar for dollar. The maximum amount that can pass tax free due to this tax credit reduction is equal to its equivalent lifetime exclusion amount.

Estate Taxes by Size of Estate

Size of Taxable Estate	Base Amount	Base Tax	Plus % on Excess over Base
$1,000,001–$1,250,000	$1,000,000	$345,800	41%
$1,250,001–$1,500,000	$1,250,000	$448,300	43%
$1,500,001–$2,000,000	$1,500,000	$555,800	45%
$2,000,001–$2,500,000	$2,000,000	$780,800	49%*
Over $2,500,000	$2,500,000	$1,025,800	50%*

** The maximum rate of tax is scheduled to be lowered. See chart on page 143.*

Assets Included in Your Gross Estate at Death

To be taxed, the assets included in your gross estate must be both *owned by you at the time of death and transferred to another.* The following are examples of assets included in your estate for estate tax purposes:

- **Real estate:** Residential, vacation property, farm or business real estate.
- **Bank accounts:** Checking, savings, CDs, money market funds.
- **Financial assets:** Stocks, bonds, treasury bills, mutual funds.
- **Money loaned to others:** Notes, mortgages, installment sales.
- **Business assets:** Equipment, tools, machinery.
- **Closely-held businesses:** Partnerships, limited liability companies, closely-held stock.
- **Personal property:** Automobiles, trucks, furniture, guns, antiques, collectibles.
- **Retirement plans:** IRAs, 401(k)s, Keoghs.
- **Annuities**
- **Life insurance:** Proceeds of life insurance on your life are included in your estate only *if they are paid to your estate or you owned the policy.* Many are surprised to learn that the life insurance policies they own on their life are included as part of their lifetime exclusion amount.
- **Jointly-owned assets:** The full value of all assets owned as joint tenants with rights of survivorship is included in the gross estate of the *first* joint owner to die. Federal estate tax rules apply a different approach to jointly-owned assets than Pennsylvania does. In Pennsylvania, only the value of the partial interest owned by the decedent is taxed. The federal government, however, taxes the *entire value of the jointly owned assets in the estate of the first joint owner to die,* unless it can

Life insurance policies are included in the lifetime exclusion amount.

be proven that some portion was paid for by survivors. (The estate tax has an exception to this rule for assets owned jointly by husband and wife. In that case, only half of the value of the joint assets is taxed in the estate of the first to die.)

Valuing the Gross Estate

Fair market value is the price at which a willing buyer would buy and a willing seller would sell.

Once all of the assets of the estate are identified, valuing the gross estate is the next step. Since the value of the estate determines the tax, an important element of estate planning is the proper valuation of assets.

All assets are valued at the fair market value as of the date of death. Fair market value is the price at which a willing buyer would buy and a willing seller would sell the assets, both having reasonable knowledge of all relevant facts and neither under any compulsion to buy or sell. There is an exception to the requirement of valuing assets as of the date of death. It is known as the ALTERNATE VALUATION DATE. This is a date six months after the date of death. Assets can be valued as of that date only if using that value results in both a lower gross estate and lower estate taxes.

SPECIAL USE VALUATION OF REAL ESTATE USED IN A FARM OR BUSINESS

If the decedent was using real estate as a farm or business for five of the eight years preceding death, there may be the option of valuing it *based on its actual use*, which may be *less* than its fair market value. The benefit of this special use valuation is limited to a maximum of $800,000 reduction in value. This amount is indexed for inflation.

The rules for this special use valuation are complex and based upon the assets qualifying as special use property. Valuation rules include the fact that the real estate must pass to a close family member (a QUALIFIED HEIR) who must continue its qualified use for a minimum of ten years. There are other requirements to qualify for this special valuation and *professional assistance is a must* to ensure all requirements are properly complied with.

Estate Tax Deductions & Credits

Once the gross estate is identified and valued, a number of deductions are permitted:

- **Debts and unpaid mortgages of the decedent.**
- **Estate settlement expenses:** Including administrative and funeral expenses, executor's fees, attorney's fees, and interest.
- **Charitable deduction:** For the value of all assets transferred by the decedent's estate to qualified charities. This deduction does not apply if gifts are made by the heirs and are not specified in the decedent's estate plan.
- **Marital deduction** (*Reviewed in depth in Chapter 7*): This deduction is for the value of all assets passing to the decedent's surviving spouse. The rules that determine whether this deduction applies are as follows:

    1. The decedent must be a U.S. citizen.
    2. The person receiving the distribution must be the decedent's surviving spouse.
    3. The assets being transferred must be included in the decedent's gross estate.
    4. The assets must pass from the decedent to the surviving spouse.

One of the provisions of The Tax Relief Act of 1997 was the introduction of the qualified family-owned business deduction.

- **Qualified family-owned business deduction:** This is a deduction of up to $1,300,000. In order to qualify, the decedent must have been a United States citizen and the value of the family-owned business must exceed 50% of the adjusted gross estate of the decedent. In addition, the business interest must have been owned by the decedent during five of the previous eight years before death. The decedent's interest must pass to a qualified heir upon the decedent's death and the family business must stay in the family for a minimum of ten years after death. As with the special use valuation, there are additional requirements to qualify for this deduction and professional assistance is a must.

Due to the complexity of the rules and the difficulties in lifetime planning to use the qualified family-owned business deduction, many estate planners suggest their clients simply purchase life insurance to provide the cash required to pay estate taxes with respect to closely-held business interests. (This deduction has been repealed for the estates of those dying after December 31, 2003.)

- **State Death Tax Credit:** There is also a tax credit equal to the value of inheritance taxes paid to Pennsylvania or other states. This credit applies only to death taxes actually paid. The state death tax credit is currently being phased out and will be terminated beginning in 2005. In its place will be a deduction from the value of the gross estate equal to the amount of Pennsylvania (and other states) inheritance taxes paid.

Payment of the Estate Tax

The estate tax is due within nine months of the date of death. Unlike Pennsylvania's inheritance tax, there is no discount for early payment of the tax.

Liquidity Planning

A significant challenge when planning for the federal estate tax is finding the cash necessary to pay it. The tax is due within *nine months of the date of death* and the IRS generally requires immediate payment in full. There are four sources of money to pay the tax:

1. Sell Estate Assets

The money to pay the tax could be raised by selling estate assets. Forced sales are generally to be avoided because they could result in receiving sales proceeds that are far below the fair market value of the assets being sold as a result of the strict time constraints.

2. Borrow the Money from the Bank or Beneficiaries

This presumes the estate has the capacity to borrow the money for, perhaps, a ten-year period at reasonable interest rates. Like forced liquidation of assets, borrowing money from the bank to pay the tax is an expensive alternative, and beneficiaries seldom have the ability or desire to loan money to an estate.

3. Borrow the Money from the IRS — Section 6166 Deferral

The executor of the estate could elect to pay the estate tax attributable to certain closely-held business interests using ten annual installments. Since the first payment does not have to be made until five years after the date of death, a total deferral period of fourteen years may result in paying the estate tax attributable to the closely-held business. (Interest expense will be incurred on the unpaid balance of the tax.)

4. Purchase Life Insurance

In many cases, the optimal choice to provide the liquidity necessary to pay the taxes is to purchase life insurance.

Overview of the Gift Tax

There is no repeal of the gift tax in 2010.

Whenever assets are given to another for less than its full value, the amount by which the value of the assets exceed the money paid for them is a gift. Although the Tax Relief Act of 2001 carries a provision to repeal the federal estate tax, *there is no repeal of the gift tax* and the gift tax top rate becomes 35% in the year 2010.

Who Must Pay the Tax?

The gift tax affects gifts that exceed the gift tax ANNUAL EXCLUSION AMOUNT. For 2002, this amount is $11,000, and it is adjusted for inflation. The first $11,000 given by a donor to any single donee in any calendar year is excluded from the gift tax. Therefore, to the extent that in any given year you give $11,000 or less to any one person, there is no gift tax. Gifts made to anyone, regardless of their relationship to the donor, qualify for the annual exclusion amount.

In addition to the $11,000 gift by an individual, husbands and wives may split gifts between them. For example, if a husband wanted to give a $22,000 gift to his nephew, his wife could join in the gift and there would be no gift tax due because it would be deemed to be a $11,000 gift from the husband and a $11,000 gift from his wife. There is also an unlimited marital deduction on gifts made by one spouse to the other so long as each spouse is a U.S. citizen.

In addition to the $11,000 annual exclusion, there is an unlimited exclusion for payments made for educational tuition expense and medical expenses. The amounts paid for educational tuition and medical expenses must be paid directly to the educational institution or the medical provider.

A gift can be any type of asset and still qualify for the $11,000 annual exclusion. It does not need to be cash. For example if Mother and Father own an $800,000 farm, they can gift a partial interest in the farm to their son by conveying to him by deed an $11,000 interest from Father and an $11,000 interest from Mother for a total $22,000 interest in the farm. This would be a deed transferring 2.75% of the farm ($22,000 ÷ $800,000). An additional portion of the farm could be conveyed if a discount is applied to the value of the gift due to its lack of marketability.

How the Gift Tax Interacts with the Estate Tax

If you give over $11,000 to any one donee, the amount exceeding $11,000 will reduce your federal estate and gift tax lifetime exclusion amount. (*See chart on page 143.*) Once you have made gifts to one individual in excess of the total of both your $11,000 annual exclusion amount and your $1,000,000 lifetime gift tax exclusion amount, you must pay gift tax on the value of the gifts in excess of this total.

The Generous Father Plans Ahead

If Jonathon gave his daughter, Jane, $50,000, a gift tax return would be required to be filed. The gift tax return would show that of the $50,000 gift from Jonathon to Jane, $11,000 qualified for the annual exclusion amount. The remaining $39,000 in gift will reduce Jonathon's federal estate tax lifetime exclusion amount to $961,000 ($1,000,000 – $39,000 = $961,000). Unlike the graduating exemption scale for the estate tax, the lifetime exclusion amount for gifts remains at $1,000,000 indefinitely.

Payment of the Gift Tax

In the event a gift tax return is due, it generally must be filed *no later than April 15 of the calendar year following the year of the gift.* If the assets being gifted are hard to value (such as farmland, real estate, or unlisted stock), it must be appraised so that the value of the gift can be confirmed.

Income Tax Problems Related to the Gift Tax

APPRECIATION IN VALUE

Although a gift tax rarely needs to be paid when making gifts, there are income tax issues to consider. A gift of assets that have appreciated in value while held by the donor can cause unplanned income tax expense to the donee.

The Generous Dad & His Wise Investment

Mitch owns stock with a fair market value of $120,000. He bought the stock twenty years ago for $20,000. The income tax basis is equal to what Mitch paid for the stock. Therefore, if he sold it, he would pay capital gains tax on $100,000, the amount of gain ($120,000 – $20,000). If, instead of selling it, Mitch gives the stock to his son, Jason, Jason would receive both the stock and Mitch's $20,000 tax basis on the stock. Thereafter, if Jason sells the stock, he will pay capital gains tax on the difference between his sale price and the $20,000 basis that he received from his father.

There is a different result, however, if Jason inherits the stock from his dad. Those receiving assets by inheritance, receive what is called a "step-up" in basis. This means that Jason would inherit Mitch's stock but, in addition, the tax basis of the stock would be the fair market value on the date of Mitch's death, or the alternate valuation date, if elected. The result is that if Jason inherits the stock, he also receives a tax basis of $120,000, the fair market value of the stock as reported by the estate. Now, if Jason sells the stock for $120,000, he pays no capital gains tax. This is a significant tax benefit that is lost when assets are gifted during one's lifetime instead of given through an estate after death.

CHANGES IN THE STEP-UP RULES

When the estate tax is repealed in 2010, the rule providing for the step-up in basis will change. The new rule will be that the step-up in basis upon death will be limited to only the first $1,300,000 of increase in the value of assets. There will be an additional $3,000,000 of step-up in basis permitted on assets inherited by a surviving spouse from the first spouse to die. For all other estate assets, the basis will equal the lesser of the decedent's basis or fair market value of the assets as of the date of death. The basis can step down but not up. *This rule is only effective during the calendar year 2010.*

Heirs will be required to keep records of the cost basis of assets inherited from their parents and grandparents in order to determine the capital gains tax if they sell inherited assets. The executor will be permitted to elect the assets to receive the stepped-up basis. For purposes of eligible basis increase, these rules do not apply to assets acquired by the decedent by gift within three years of death.

The Generation-Skipping Transfer Tax

When the federal estate tax was imposed, families began to avoid it by making gifts to their *grand*children instead of to their children. This strategy avoided the tax that would occur when their children would transfer the same wealth to their grandchildren. They could thereby skip a generation. The government responded to this planning technique, and The Tax Reform Act of 1986 instituted the GENERATION-SKIPPING TRANSFER TAX. This is a tax imposed upon the value of assets transferred from one generation to a succeeding generation, only if it skips a generation in between. The tax is designed to produce the same result as though the estate tax had been imposed on the transfer to each successive generation.

A generation-skipping transfer occurs when any transfer of assets skips a generation.

A generation-skipping transfer occurs when any transfer of assets skips a generation. Skips can be direct skips, where assets are left directly to grandchildren, or an indirect skip where assets are transferred into a trust for the benefit of a child, and only upon the child's death, trust assets are transferred to grandchildren.

There is an exemption from the generation-skipping transfer tax. The exemption is indexed for inflation. For 2002 the exemption is $1,100,000. The tax rate is the same as the highest estate tax rate on amounts transferred in excess of the lifetime exemption amount.

Summary

Since 1916 the federal estate tax has been a part of life for many Americans. Although the current lifetime exclusion amount from this tax is $1 million dollars, it is important that you carefully consider whether or not your estate will ever be exposed to this tax. Indeed, since the current law repeals the tax for only one year, 2010, all of us need to be prepared for its possible return in 2011.

9

How To Reduce the Federal Estate Tax

Topics Include

Five Primary Strategies To Reduce or Eliminate the Tax:

1. The Unlimited Marital Deduction

2. Credit Shelter Trusts

3. Lifetime Gifts to Family

4. Discounting the Value of Assets

5. Prepay the Tax with Life Insurance

Introduction

THERE ARE DOZENS OF STRATEGIES to minimize the FEDERAL ESTATE TAXES families must pay, many outside the scope of this book. In this chapter, we will look at five primary estate planning strategies. Not all of these strategies will apply to every reader. On the other hand, there may be readers with estates that are large enough to justify an approach more complex than the strategies discussed here. Yet, these are the five strategies that must be addressed before pushing ahead into more complex planning.

Strategy Number One: Maximize the Unlimited Marital Deduction

Unlike the federal income tax with its numerous deductions, there are few deductions from the federal *estate* tax. Of the deductions available, there are only two that lend themselves to significant planning strategies. They are the MARITAL DEDUCTION, and the charitable deduction. This section examines the marital deduction and its impact on saving tax dollars. (*The charitable deduction is covered in detail in Chapter 10.*)

HOW TO QUALIFY FOR THE UNLIMITED MARITAL DEDUCTION

The unlimited marital deduction is applied to estate assets that pass from the deceased spouse to the surviving spouse. The first spouse to pass away must be a U.S. citizen or a resident of the United States. In addition, the surviving spouse must be a citizen of the United States to qualify for the unlimited marital deduction. In the event that the surviving spouse is *not* a U.S. citizen, a limited marital deduction is permitted by using what is known as a QUALIFIED DOMESTIC TRUST.

The unlimited marital deduction is applied to estate assets that pass from the deceased spouse to the surviving spouse.

FORMS OF TRANSFER THAT QUALIFY FOR THE MARITAL DEDUCTION

Outright transfers of assets to the surviving spouse qualify for the marital deduction. In addition to outright transfer, there are a number of trusts that qualify for the marital deduction when the deceased spouse transfers assets into a trust. These trusts are known as MARITAL TRUSTS, and include the power of appointment trust, the Q-TIP TRUST, and the qualified domestic trust mentioned earlier.

The 2 Primary Deductions Allowed under Federal Estate Tax Law Are :

1. **The Marital Deduction** (Trusts that qualify for the marital deduction)
   - Power of Appointment Trust: Allows the surviving spouse the greatest control over how trust assets will be distributed after his death.
   - Q-TIP Trust: More options with regard to post-mortem estate planning. The surviving spouse does not have the power to change the ultimate distribution regarding who receives the Q-TIP trust assets after the surviving spouse's death.
   - Qualified Domestic Trust: Used to apply the marital deduction to a non-U.S. citizen surviving spouse.
2. **The Charitable Deduction** (*See Chapter 10.*)

Power of Appointment Trust

The power of appointment trust *allows the surviving spouse the greatest control over how trust assets will be distributed after her death.* A trust will qualify as a power of appointment trust so long as the surviving spouse is entitled to *all* the income at least annually for life. In addition, no person other than the surviving spouse may receive a distribution from the trust during the surviving spouse's lifetime. The surviving spouse must have a general power to appoint the assets to anyone after her death. This means that the surviving spouse may specify in her will or living trust who shall receive the remaining assets in the trust after her death. In addition, the surviving spouse may be given the right to make gifts from the power of appointment trust during her lifetime. The power of appointment trust also permits the trustee to pay as much of the principal to the surviving spouse as the trustee deems advisable or as requested by the surviving spouse.

The power of appointment trust is often used when a spouse believes that if he were to die first, the surviving spouse does not have the experience or desire to manage trust assets. In order to provide management for trust assets, this spouse establishes a power of appointment trust that permits the surviving spouse to distribute trust assets to whomever he chooses when he dies. If the surviving spouse does not name the new trust beneficiaries in his will or living trust, as permitted by the trust, the distribution plan in the power of appointment trust will be effective.

Q-TIP Trust

Q-TIP stands for QUALIFIED TERMINAL INTEREST PROPERTY. This trust is similar to the power of appointment trust. The main difference is that *the surviving spouse does not have the power to change the ultimate distribution regarding who receives the Q-TIP trust assets after her death.* The surviving spouse must receive all of the income at least annually for life from the Q-TIP trust. Unlike the power of appointment trust, the assets cannot be controlled by the will or living trust of the surviving spouse. The first spouse established the terms regarding who receives the trust assets after the death of the surviving spouse, and no one else may have a power of appointment over trust assets during the surviving spouse's lifetime. This trust is used more than the power of appointment trust.

Q-TIP trusts will continue to be an important estate planning tool to provide income to the surviving spouse while protecting the principal for the decedent's beneficiaries.

Another significant difference between the power of appointment trust and the Q-TIP trust is that the power of appointment trust, when properly drafted, *automatically* qualifies for the marital deduction; whereas a Q-TIP election must be made to qualify all or only a portion of the Q-TIP trust for the marital deduction. This gives the executor options with regard to post-mortem estate planning. The Q-TIP trust is used when one spouse wishes to provide for independent management of trust assets for the surviving spouse as well as control the final disposition of trust assets upon the surviving spouse's death.

Depending upon the decedent's wishes, the trustee may or may not be given the option to invade principal for the benefit of the surviving spouse. Since the entire value of the Q-TIP trust is included in the surviving spouse's estate at his death, there are no limitations on invading principal for his benefit. Full access to principal may be provided to the surviving spouse for any reason. If, however, the purpose of the Q-TIP trust is to protect the ultimate beneficiaries' interest (deceased spouse's children from a prior marriage, for example), then the provisions to invade the principal should be somewhat restricted. Since the federal

Forget It, Larry

Mr White's first wife and the mother of his two sons died years ago. White remarried, but had no children with the second Mrs. White.

As a successful investor, White was concerned about what would happen to his estate upon his death, and subsequently, his wife's. While his wife had no children, she did have a brother, Larry. When his wife dies, Mr White wants his estate to pass to his sons, not to Larry; therefore, White set up a Q-TIP trust to specify where and to whom his assets go after he and Mrs. White die.

estate tax lifetime exclusion amount is increasing to $3.5 million, and full repeal is scheduled for the year 2010, Q-TIP trusts may not be necessary in many estates solely for estate tax planning purposes. Q-TIP trusts, however, will continue to be an important estate planning tool for those who wish to provide income to the surviving spouse while protecting the principal for the decedent's beneficiaries.

Qualified Domestic Trust

For the marital deduction to apply for non-U.S. citizen surviving spouses, a special type of trust must be used.

In the late 1980s, Congress was concerned with the possibility that a U.S. citizen would die, leaving his entire estate to his non–U. S. citizen spouse , who could then use the marital deduction and take the assets back to her native country. In this scenario, the estate would never be taxed. In 1988, Congress changed the estate tax law to correct this problem. Now, in order for the marital deduction to apply for non–U.S. citizen surviving spouses, a special type of trust must be used as a marital trust. This trust is known as a qualified domestic trust or Q-DOT.

This trust is only necessary to the extent that the first spouse that dies has an estate greater than that year's lifetime exemption amount. For example, a husband is a U.S. citizen and has assets registered solely in his name equal to $1,000,000. He dies in 2002 and gives everything to his wife. Since his total estate is equal to his lifetime exemption amount, this amount is permitted to be distributed directly to his non-citizen spouse. On the other hand, to the extent his assets are greater than the lifetime exemption amount, the only way to avoid paying federal estate tax is to have the decedent's assets transferred to a qualified domestic trust. At least one trustee of the qualified domestic trust must be a citizen of the United States or a domestic corporation.

SHOULD THE TRANSFER TO YOUR SURVIVING SPOUSE BE OUTRIGHT OR IN TRUST?

There are a number of factors to consider when making the decision whether to transfer assets directly to your surviving spouse or transfer them into a trust for his or her benefit:

1. **Estate size:** If the total estate of both spouses does not warrant planning for the federal estate tax, the use of a trust for tax purposes would not be needed.
2. **Citizenship of the spouses:** The qualified domestic trust is a requirement in order to preserve the marital deduction on assets passing to a non-citizen spouse. If the total estate of husband and wife is greater than the lifetime exclusion amount, the qualified domestic trust is needed if one is not a U.S. citizen.
3. **Management abilities of the surviving spouse:** At times, no federal estate tax planning is needed, but there is concern about the ability of the surviving spouse to manage assets previously controlled by the deceased spouse. In this situation, a Q-TIP trust or power of appointment trust should be considered. This would permit a qualified trustee to manage trust assets for the benefit of the surviving spouse and still qualify for the marital deduction.
4. **Possible remarriage of the surviving spouse:** If the first spouse to die leaves everything outright to the surviving spouse (and the surviving spouse remarries), it is possible that upon the death of surviving spouse the new spouse would receive the inheritance and the children of the deceased spouse would be disinherited.

When there is concern about the ability of the surviving spouse to manage assets, a Q-TIP trust or power of appointment trust should be considered.

Strategy Number Two: A Credit Shelter Trust "Saves" the Lifetime Exclusion Amount of the First Spouse to Die

As discussed in Chapter 8, every U.S. citizen has a lifetime exclusion amount. This is the amount that can pass free of federal estate tax at death. Since a husband and wife each have their own lifetime exclusion amount, in the year 2002 each can pass $1,000,000 of their estate tax free to their heirs, for a total tax-free transfer of $2,000,000. Unfortunately, if no prior planning is done, there is a catch to this lifetime exclusion amount for for married taxpayers: If it is not used during lifetime or *at death*, it is lost.

BENEFITS OF THE CREDIT SHELTER TRUST

If the lifetime exclusion amount is not used during lifetime or at death, it is lost.

The primary benefit of the credit shelter trust (also known as a BYPASS TRUST or an AB TRUST) is the federal estate tax savings it offers. If husband and wife have each established a credit shelter trust in their will or living trust (and have appropriately registered their assets), they can together transfer up to $2,000,000 to their family and heirs with no federal estate tax. The lifetime exclusion amount is scheduled to increase: By the year 2009, a husband and wife will be able to transfer up to $7,000,000 to the next generation with no federal estate tax, provided they engage in planning.

HOW CREDIT SHELTER TRUSTS ARE ESTABLISHED

Credit shelter trust language can be written into either a will or living trust. Since no one knows which spouse will pass away first, the language is placed in each spouse's will or living trust. The will or living trust of the first spouse to die is the only one that will have its credit shelter trust established, since the trust is always established for the benefit of a surviving spouse. When the surviving spouse passes away, no credit shelter trust is necessary in order to take advantage of the full lifetime exclusion amount available to the surviving spouse.

Use It or Lose It

Bill and Estelle had been married for thirty years and had grown their estate to $2,000,000 when Bill suddenly passed away. There were no federal estate taxes on Bill's assets transferred to Estelle because they qualified for the marital deduction.

Unfortunately, Bill's $1,000,000 lifetime exclusion amount was lost because he never used it during his lifetime, nor did he create an estate plan to utilize it after his death. As a result, when Estelle dies, she can pass only $1 million of the estate (the amount of her lifetime exclusion) tax free to her heirs (if she dies in 2002 or 2003). This would result in over $300,000 in federal estate taxes that could have been avoided.

By sheltering Bill's lifetime exclusion amount in a credit shelter trust, Bill and Estelle together would have been able to pass their $2 million estate tax free to their children.

CHOOSING THE TRUSTEE OF THE CREDIT SHELTER TRUST

The surviving spouse is permitted to be trustee of the credit shelter trust so long as the trust permits it. The risk is that the amount in the credit shelter trust would be includible in the estate of the surviving spouse if he were to die. If the surviving spouse had been treating the credit shelter trust assets as his own money, it would be taxed. If the trust is carefully drafted, and the surviving spouse follows the guidelines, the trust will not be included in the estate of the second spouse to die. Of course, the surviving spouse is *not required* to be the trustee and often it is preferable to name a bank or trust company as the trustee.

HOW THE CREDIT SHELTER TRUST OPERATES

At the death of the first spouse, a will or living trust does not transfer everything outright to the surviving spouse. Instead, a will or living trust requires that a *portion of the estate* be transferred into a credit shelter trust.

The amount of the estate transferred into the credit shelter trust will be equal to that year's lifetime exclusion amount. Once the credit shelter trust has this amount transferred into it, all other assets that the first spouse owned could be given outright to the surviving spouse.

Once the lifetime exclusion amount has been transferred into the trust, all of the first spouse's other assets could be given outright to the surviving spouse.

During the surviving spouse's lifetime, he is entitled to a number of benefits from the trust:

- **Income:** During the surviving spouse's lifetime, distribution of trust income will be made according to the terms of the trust. The surviving spouse can be entitled to receive all of the income or income distributions may be left to the discretion of the trustee.
- **Principal:** Although income may be paid out to the surviving spouse without restriction, the principal must have restrictions on its use, if the surviving spouse is the trustee. In that case, distribution of principal must be restricted to an ASCERTAINABLE STANDARD that limits distributions to amounts required for the surviving spouse's health, education, maintenance or support. If the trustee is a bank or trust company, the trust provisions can give broad discretionary powers to the trustee to distribute principal to the surviving spouse.
- **"5 & 5" Provision:** This provision permits the trustee to invade the principal of the trust and pay it to the surviving spouse in an amount limited to the greater of 5% of the value of the trust principal or $5,000. This is a limit on the power the surviving spouse may have to invade principal for reasons in addition to ascertainable standards. The reason for the limit is that if the surviving spouse has the ability to make withdrawals greater than this amount without standards, the IRS would include the value of the credit shelter trust in the estate of the surviving spouse for federal estate tax purposes.

REGISTERING ASSETS TO FUND THE CREDIT SHELTER TRUST

In order to enable the lifetime exclusion amount of the first spouse to die to be transferred into his or her credit shelter trust, the assets must be registered in the sole name of the first spouse to die. Even with the credit shelter trust language carefully written into his will or living trust, if the husband dies first and has no assets registered in his sole name, the credit shelter trust may not be funded. For example, if husband and wife own a home and investment accounts jointly and if the husband names his wife the beneficiary of his IRA and life insurance, there are no assets available to be fully transferred into the husband's credit shelter trust (unless the surviving spouse uses the disclaimer strategies as discussed on page 168).

If the husband dies first and has no assets registered in his sole name, the credit shelter trust may not be funded.

As stated earlier, the estate planning process is not complete without carefully reviewing the registration of all assets. All designated beneficiaries and contingent beneficiaries must be closely reviewed as well. This includes annuities, IRAs, and transfer on death (T.O.D.) accounts. (*The use of beneficiary designations to fund the credit shelter trust is covered in more detail in Chapter 6.*)

In addition to the challenges of locating assets that can be easily re-registered, there are emotional considerations. For example, if a wife had inherited a substantial amount of telephone company stock from her parents, how would she feel about re-registering her inheritance into the sole name of her husband? By the same token, a husband, or wife, might feel that upon re-registering a large amount of assets into the name of their spouse, he or she might not be able to cope with managing the assets.

Exceptions to the Rule

There have been recent developments in Pennsylvania relating to the legality of the surviving spouse to disclaim his or her interest in jointly held assets after the death of his or her spouse. These recent developments make it possible to fund the credit shelter trust of the first spouse to die even if all assets were owned jointly. (*Review the discussion on disclaimers in Chapter 2.*)

Calculating the Value of Assets Needed To Fund a Credit Shelter Trust

There are a number of strategies used to fund the credit shelter trust of the first spouse to die. Since the purpose of the credit shelter trust is to utilize the lifetime exclusion amount of the first spouse to die, the concept is to fund it with the *minimum* amount necessary to avoid all federal estate tax at the time the surviving spouse dies. Therefore, married taxpayers whose total estates are less than the $1 million lifetime exclusion amount for 2002 do not need a credit shelter trust. For larger estates, however, it becomes necessary to calculate the appropriate portion of the estate that should be used to fund the credit shelter trust of the first spouse to die. The fact that the value of the lifetime exclusion amount is increasing over the course of the next several years makes funding the credit shelter trust particularly challenging. We will now consider the following strategies, which are used to fund a credit shelter trust.

Mandatory Funding

Mandatory funding refers to the language placed in the will or living trust. When mandatory funding is used, the estate planning documents *require* the funding of the credit shelter trust. The document directs the executor or trustee to transfer an amount equal to the lifetime exclusion amount into the credit shelter trust. Using the mandatory funding strategy requires that assets be titled correctly during lifetime and the estate planner and client have specifically identified the assets that will fund the credit shelter trust, regardless of which spouse would pass away first.

Estate plans with mandatory funding need to be updated regularly to reflect changes in the lifetime exclusion amount.

Caution must be used with mandatory funding because of the increases scheduled in the amount of the lifetime exclusion amount. Estate plans with mandatory funding need to be updated regularly to reflect the changes in the amount. The potential problem is that the first spouse to pass away will have a will or living trust requiring the credit shelter trust to be funded in an amount equal to that year's lifetime exemption amount, and the credit shelter trust may not even be necessary if the federal estate tax was repealed or if the estate size of both spouses has fallen below the lifetime exclusion amount.

Funding the Marital Trust before the Credit Shelter Trust

As mentioned above, the challenge with funding the credit shelter trust is the fact that until the date of death (or permanent repeal of federal estate tax) no one will know the value of the lifetime exclusion amount that will apply at the time of their death. For this reason, it is important to consider the possibility that the value of the decedent's estate at the time of death could be less than his lifetime exclusion amount for that year. If a married couple has a total estate that is less than the lifetime exclusion amount at the time the first spouse dies, and if the credit shelter trust is funded first (because the will or living trust specifies mandatory funding), all of the assets of the first spouse to die will be used to fund the credit shelter trust when, for tax purposes, no credit shelter trust is needed. This could result in some hardship if the surviving spouse does not have adequate assets in his or her own name.

The total lifetime exclusion amount of the first spouse to die may not be used to be certain that sufficient assets are available to the surviving spouse.

One approach to minimize this negative result is to have a will or a living trust direct that before any assets go into the credit shelter trust, the deceased spouse's assets are given outright (or in trust) to the surviving spouse to the extent necessary so that the surviving spouse's total taxable estate is equal to the current lifetime exclusion amount. Only after this has been accomplished can the balance of the estate of the first spouse to die be allocated to the credit shelter trust.

With a plan of this nature, if the estate tax is repealed or the lifetime exclusion amount exceeds a couple's total estate value, there will be no funding of the credit shelter trust. Funding the marital trust, or giving the deceased spouse's assets outright to the surviving spouse, before the credit shelter trust is funded should only be used with careful consideration since it intentionally allows for underfunding the credit shelter trust. As a result, the total lifetime exclusion amount of the first spouse to die may not be used to be certain that sufficient assets are available to the surviving spouse. This approach should be considered when the total taxable estate of both spouses does not exceed their total lifetime exclusion amount, and it is not expected to exceed that amount during their lifetime. If the disclaimer method is not used (as we are about to discuss), this technique will confirm that no estate assets are distributed to the credit shelter trust until the surviving spouse has the equivalent of the current lifetime exclusion amount in her own name.

Funding the Marital Trust First

Susan and Marty have a total estate of $1,500,000 and each has $750,000 titled in his or her sole name. Marty dies with a taxable estate of $750,000. The current lifetime exclusion amount is $1 million. Funding the marital trust before the credit shelter trust will require that only $250,000 of Marty's estate would need to be allocated to the marital share (as a result of which Susan's estate now totals $1 million) and only Marty's remaining $500,000 will be used to fund Marty's credit shelter trust. This results in the intentional underfunding of Marty's credit shelter trust in order to keep as much flexibility as possible in Susan's estate. If mandatory funding had been used, Marty's credit shelter trust would have been fully funded up to $750,000 when it would not have required that much to zero out federal estate tax, upon his wife's subsequent death.

Disclaimer Funding

Another strategy to fund a credit shelter trust is the use of DISCLAIMERS. Disclaiming is more flexible than mandatory funding. For example, if the estate should shrink below the lifetime exclusion amount for any given year, the disclaimer technique would ensure that the credit shelter trust would not be funded, since it would not be necessary.

When using disclaimers to fund the credit shelter trust, the deceased spouse's will or living trust must state that that the entire estate is to be paid to the surviving spouse. As a result, the surviving spouse has the option to disclaim any or all of the interest transferred to him or her from the deceased spouse's estate. Disclaimed assets are transferred into the credit shelter trust instead of being given to the surviving spouse. Since partial disclaimers are permitted, disclaimers are helpful because of the increasing amount of the lifetime exclusion amount. As the value of the lifetime exclusion amount increases, the surviving spouse has the flxibility to direct lesser amounts into the credit shelter trust to save federal estate taxes upon his or her subsequent death. Using disclaimer language in the will or living trust also means that if the federal estate tax is repealed, there will be no need to change the will or living trust. This is because disclaimer language transfers everything to the surviving spouse outright, and there would be no need for subsequent disclaiming to reduce estate taxes.

When using disclaimers to fund the credit shelter trust, the deceased spouse's will or living trust must state that the entire estate is to be paid to the surviving spouse.

A disadvantage to disclaimers is the rigid rules concerning disclaiming. The surviving spouse must not "accept any benefit" from the asset to be disclaimed in order to disclaim it. If income is received or other benefits accepted, the assets that generated the income may not be available for disclaimer. For example, if all dividends from stock of the first spouse to die are automatically deposited into a joint checking account and the surviving spouse uses the joint checking account to pay bills, this will have an impact on the ability to disclaim the stock. Another difficulty with disclaimers is that when a spouse dies, he or she is depending upon the surviving spouse to take action at the appropriate time and voluntarily give up her right to absolute control over the disclaimed assets.

Clayton Q-TIP

As the lifetime exclusion amount increases over the next few years, if mandatory funding is used, more and more of the estate of the first spouse to die will be held in the credit shelter trust. Since it is impossible to know what the lifetime exclusion amount will be when the first spouse dies, it is important to build as much flexibility as possible into the estate plan so that only the minimum required goes into the credit shelter trust, in addition to funding the marital trust first, as described previously. A flexible approach to keeping options open is the use of a Clayton Q-TIP trust. The Clayton Q-TIP trust permits the executor of the estate of the deceased spouse to allocate a portion of the estate to the credit shelter trust. The portion allocated to the credit shelter trust is the portion of the Clayton Q-TIP for which the marital deduction is not elected. In effect, the executor calculates the optimum amount to be held in the credit shelter trust to minimize the taxes due when the surviving spouse dies. The executor then elects to have a portion of the deceased spouse's estate equal to that amount transferred to the credit shelter trust. The balance of the decedent's estate will be held in a Q-TIP trust qualifying for the marital deduction.

This ability to defer the final decision as to the allocation of assets between the marital trust and the credit shelter trust until after the death of the first spouse to die is very flexible. This approach also gives a great deal of authority to the executor. The surviving spouse should not be given the authority to make this determination, it should be exercised by a bank or trust company.

> This approach has a number of advantages over the strategy of disclaiming. One advantage is that the rigid requirements for disclaiming are not required to be observed when using a Clayton Q-TIP trust. In addition, a disclaimer must be made within nine months of the date of death. The Q-TIP election can be made up to fifteen months after the date of death if the estate files for an extension on the estate tax return.

Strategy Number Three: Make Lifetime Gifts to Family Members

We've discussed two strategies, so far, to minimize federal estate taxes: 1) use the marital deductions, and 2), use both spouses' lifetime exclusion amounts. The third strategy is to *remove assets from your taxable estate.*

We will now review the strategy of making gifts during your lifetime; gifts that will remove assets from your estate. We will also consider the use of life insurance trusts to remove the death benefit of life insurance from your estate.

A systematic lifetime gifting program lowers the federal estate tax, because there is generally no federal estate tax on gifts given during lifetime. As discussed in Chapter 8, the gift tax has an annual exclusion

There is generally no federal estate tax on gifts given during lifetime.

amount of $11,000. Thus, the first $11,000 of gifts given by a donor to any single donee in any calendar year is tax free. Husband and wife can give a total of $22,000 to each of their children or any other individual. If any single donee receives an amount over $11,000 from one donor, a gift tax return is required and it would reduce the lifetime exclusion amount to the extent the gift is over $11,000.

How to Reduce Estate Assets Using Systematic Lifetime Giving

The use of this strategy can be illustrated by considering a couple with three children. Since the parents can give $22,000 per year to each child, they would be able to reduce their estate by $66,000 each calendar year. If each of their three children were married, gifts could be made to the spouses of their children also, resulting in gifts of $132,000 given each year to reduce the taxable estate of the parents.

Gifting & the Capital Gains Tax

The capital gains tax must be considered when making gifts. This is because the recipient receives the same CARRY-OVER BASIS as the giver of the gift.

Balancing the capital gains tax and federal estate tax must be considered when gifted assets have a low basis relative to its current market value. Since the highest rate of the capital gains tax is 20%, and the highest rate of the federal estate tax is 50%, sometimes gifting low basis assets is a good strategy to avoid the federal estate tax. On the other hand, if there will be no federal estate tax due, but only Pennsylvania inheritance tax, one must balance the difference between a 20% capital gains tax versus only a 4.5% Pennsylvania inheritance tax. In such cases it may be more beneficial not to gift low basis assets, but to pass them out of the estate at death as an inheritance and pay the 4.5% inheritance tax.

Gifts to Minors

Giving gifts to minors has a few challenges since one must be at least eighteen years old to legally receive a gift. Three options for giving gifts to minors are as follows:

From Father to Son

Scott inherited stock from his father back in 1960. At that time, the stock was worth $2 per share. Today, the stock is worth $20 per share. If Scott gives the stock to his teenage son, Jerry, Jerry's basis in the stock is the same as his dad's, $2 per share. This means that if Jerry decides to sell the stock, he must pay capital gains tax on the difference in value between his dad's basis ($2) and the money Jerry receives for the stock upon its sale.

On the other hand, if Jerry had received his dad's stock as an inheritance from Scott's estate, the stock would have received a "step-up" in basis. (This means that assets received from the estate of a decedent has a new cost basis equal to the fair market value of the assets on the date of death of the decedent.) Jerry's basis would be $20 per share (if he inherits the stock). Therefore, if Jerry were to sell the stock for $20 per share after receiving it from his father's estate, he would pay no capital gains tax.

The Pennsylvania Uniform Transfer to Minors Act (PUTMA)

PUTMA provides a simple option for making gifts to minors. This strategy is applicable where either the donor, the minor, or the custodian is a resident of Pennsylvania. Gifts under PUTMA are made by transferring the gift to a CUSTODIAN. The custodian is the one responsible to manage the funds in the account for the benefit of the minor. An account may be established for only one minor and only one person may serve as the custodian. Transfers to the custodian are *irrevocable* and the assets are then considered to be owned by the minor, subject to the management authority of the custodian.

For income tax purposes, the minor is considered the owner of the assets and, therefore, income from the assets is reported on the minor's social security number. For estate and gift tax purposes, the custodial account qualifies as a completed gift for purposes of using the $11,000 annual exclusion amount. Parents must keep in mind, however, that if they serve as the custodian of a PUTMA account for their children, the value of the custodial account will be included in their estate for federal estate tax purposes.

> The custodian has the duty to manage the assets for the benefit of the minor in such fashion as the custodian considers reasonable and necessary. The custodianship ends when the minor reaches age twenty-one, at which time account assets must be given to the minor.

TRUSTS FOR MINORS

Section 2503(c)

The Internal Revenue Code provides a type of trust for making gifts to minors. Contributions to these trusts qualify for the $11,000 annual exclusion amount as long as the trust meets the following three requirements:

1. Assets transferred to the trust (and any income generated) must be used for the benefit of the minor. These trusts may have no restrictions on the power of the trustee to use trust assets for the benefit of the minor.
2. Once the minor reaches age twenty-one, whatever is in the trust must be given to the minor.
3. If the minor dies before reaching age twenty-one, the balance of the trust must be paid to his or her estate.

A drawback to the 2503(c) trust is that when the minor reaches age twenty-one the entire value of the trust *must* be given to the minor (just like a PUTMA account). One strategy to address this is to have a provision in the trust that states once the minor reaches the age of twenty-one, he or she has a thirty-day window of time in which to request that the trust assets be paid to him or her. If the minor makes no request within that window of time, the window then closes and the trust holds the assets until a later time, determined by the trust maker at the time the trust is created, such as age thirty-five or forty.

The Crummey Trust

The Crummey trust can have provisions that would pay the trust principal to the beneficiary at any age.

The Crummey trust is named after a court case involving a family whose name was Crummey. This type of trust provides that, every time a contribution is made to the trust, the trustee is required to notify all beneficiaries of the contribution. The notice gives the trust beneficiaries a limited period of time (thirty days for example) within which to instruct the trustee to pay the contribution to them. Any money that the beneficiaries do not withdraw will remain in the trust subject to the terms of the trust. The reason for the window of time for the beneficiaries to withdraw the contribution is so that the contribution to the trust qualifies as a present interest gift. This is important because for gifts to qualify for the donor's $11,000 annual exclusion amount, they must be present interest gifts. This opportunity to withdraw trust contributions is known as a CRUMMEY POWER.

Once the gift is in the trust, it is not includible in the estate of the one making the gift because of the Crummey withdrawal power given to trust beneficiaries. Unlike other strategies for making gifts to minors, the Crummey trust is not required to pay its trust assets to the minors once they reach age twenty-one. Indeed, the Crummey trust can have provisions that would pay the trust principal to the beneficiary *at any age.*

One disadvantage of the Crummey trust is the administrative requirement of issuing the Crummey withdrawal letters to the minor's guardian (or directly to the minor once he reaches age 18). The guardian must then notify the trustee whether or not the guardian will take the contribution for the benefit of the minor. Another disadvantage is that the Crummey trust must file its own income tax return each year, as the 2503(c) trust must also do, and pay income tax at the trust income tax rates on any income that is not distributed. Any income distributed to the minor beneficiaries would be taxed at the beneficiary's income tax rate. The Crummey trust is covered in more detail in the section concerning irrevocable life insurance trusts.

Section 529 College Savings Plans

Section 529 was added to the Internal Revenue Code in 1996. This section of the Code contains what is formally called a qualified tuition plan. It is also called a Section 529 plan or a 529 college savings plan. A Section 529 plan is available to all individuals regardless of income or tax bracket. Once contributions have been made to such a plan, *the earnings inside the plan will grow tax deferred.*

> Withdrawals from Section 529 college savings plans are completely free of income tax so long as the withdrawals are used for qualified higher education expenses, which include tuition, books and supplies required by a beneficiary at an eligible educational institution.
>
> Qualified higher education expenses also include reasonable costs incurred by the beneficiary for room and board. An eligible educational institution is restricted to post-secondary educational institutions. Most plans can only be used for undergraduate study at any accredited institution of higher learning within the United States.

What makes Section 529 plans so remarkable is that you (the account owner) can retain control over distributions from the account. Contributions to the plan may only be made in cash. The plan requires a designated beneficiary to be named; you and the beneficiary of the plan are prohibited from directing the investment of the capital in the plan. Your contributions to the plan are revocable, meaning that you can get your money back, but only if you pay the income taxes and a 10% penalty on the earnings. Despite this flexibility, contributions are considered completed gifts and the amounts deposited in a Section 529 plan are removed from your estate for federal estate tax purposes. Prior to the creation of Section 529 plans, the federal government did not permit revocable gifts as a way to reduce one's estate. Contributions to 529 plans qualify for the $11,000 annual exclusion amount. In addition, an election is available that permits you to "front end" these plans with as much as $55,000 (representing five years of annual gifts of $11,000). A married couple would be able to start a Section 529 plan with as much as $112,000, while inside the Section 529 plan, income grows tax-deferred.

Prior to the creation of Section 529 plans, the federal government did not permit revocable gifts as a way to reduce one's estate.

The beneficiary will only get distributions from the plan when you authorize the release of funds. In addition, the beneficiary can be changed at any time to another family member.

In regard to gifting to minors, the Section 529 plan has a number of advantages over the 2503(c) trust. The initial legal and accounting expense for establishing a trust can be avoided by making gifts to a Section 529 plan. In addition, the assets in the 2503(c) trust are required to be distributed to the minor upon reaching age 21. Contributions to a 2503(c) trust are also irrevocable. The advantages of the 2503(c) trust over the Section 529 plan include the ability of the trustee to actively manage the trust assets. In addition, the assets of the 2503(c) trust can be used for any purpose for the benefit of the minor, not just college education.

In comparison to the PENNSYLVANIA UNIFORM TRANSFER TO MINOR'S ACT, the Section 529 plan has a number of advantages as well. First, the account earnings inside a Section 529 plan grow on a tax-deferred basis, while the PUTMA earnings are taxed. In addition, with a Section 529 plan, the beneficiaries can be changed, while this is not possible with the PUTMA account. Lastly, the contributor to a Section 529 plan controls the timing of withdrawals. In contrast, when a child reaches age 21, a PUTMA account must be closed and distributed to him or her. Section 529 plans are unbeatable if the goal is that the money contributed to the plan is to be used exclusively for college expenses. If you use a Section 529 plan, it is important to state in your will or trust who shall inherit the plan in the event of your death.

Strategy Number Four: Discounting the Remaining Asset Value in Your Estate

Once the deductions have been fully planned for, the lifetime exclusion amount is protected, and assets have been removed and can no longer be included in your taxable estate, the fourth strategy is to discount the value of those assets that remain in your estate. Here, we examine the

FAMILY LIMITED PARTNERSHIP. We will also have a brief discussion on the discount that is available for a minority interest in a business.

WHAT IS A FAMILY LIMITED PARTNERSHIP?

A family limited partnership (FLP) is a business entity established to segregate and identify specific ownership interests in partnership assets for family members. Once you have carefully considered and maximized the first three strategies, if your heirs would still have federal estate taxes to pay, an FLP then becomes important to consider. Generally, parents are the general partners (maintaining control of the partnership) and the children are the limited partners, receiving only a nominal income interest during the parents' lifetime.

Creating an FLP minimizes the exposure of assets to federal estate taxes.

The general partner has full management and control over all partnership assets, and determines when and if any money is distributed to the limited partners. The general partner is entitled to a management fee for managing the partnership.

The limited partners have no management authority. The terms of the partnership agreement will limit the transferability of partnership interests so that limited partnership units cannot be bought, sold or transferred without the prior authorization of the general partner.

THE BENEFITS OF A FAMILY LIMITED PARTNERSHIP

Make Gifts to Children, but Maintain Control over the Gifted Assets

The general partner of an FLP controls the partnership. After establishing an FLP, if the parents, as general partners, make gifts to their children of only limited partnership units, the parents can still maintain complete control over the partnership and its assets. They are making gifts to their children that qualify for the $11,000 annual exclusion amount, but maintaining control over all aspects of the underlying assets. The general partner also controls the timing and the amount of distributions of income from the partnership.

Discount the Remaining Asset Value in your Estate to Your Partners

The value of any limited partnership units that the general partner owns at death can be discounted, due to the gifting of limited partnership

An Example of a Limited Family Partnership

Mr. and Mrs. Jones own an eight-unit apartment building worth $500,000. After establishing the Jones Family Limited Partnership, the apartment building is conveyed by deed by Mr. and Mrs. Jones into the name of the Jones Family Limited Partnership.

Mr. and Mrs. Jones now own 100% of the partnership, 2% as general partners and 98% as limited partners. Over the years, the Joneses gift the limited partnership interests to their children, thereby removing a significant portion of the value of the apartment building from their estate. They keep the general partnership interests in order to maintain management control of the partnership.

interests to children during lifetime. This results in lowering the federal estate tax on the partnership interest retained by the one who established the FLP.

Creditors of the Limited Partners Cannot Attach the Assets of the FLP

Not only are gifts of partnership interest given to children at a discounted value, but the gifts of limited partnership interest are sheltered from the children's creditors as well.

The personal assets of general partners, however, are not protected from creditors. For this reason, many families establish an S corporation or a limited liability company to serve as the general partner of their FLP.

Discount the Value of Gifts to Children

The value of gifts of limited partnership interest can be discounted so that a donor can transfer a greater value of assets in a shorter period of time by making gifts of limited partnership units than he could by making gifts of the underlying asset itself.

Advantages over Trusts

The FLP has two advantages over trusts. First, the accounting requirements for partnerships are less restrictive than the accounting necessary for trusts. In addition, the trustee of a trust is held to a higher standard regarding investment vehicles than the general partner of a limited partnership.

How Family Limited Partnerships Are Established

A limited partnership agreement is prepared describing in detail the rights and responsibilities of all partners. Typically a mother and father would hold 2% of the partnership as general partners. They would also initially hold the remaining 98% as limited partners.

The assets of the partnership must be valued by a qualified business valuation expert.

After the limited partnership agreement is signed by all partners and a certificate of limited partnership is filed with the Pennsylvania Department of State, assets are transferred to the partnership in exchange for both general and limited partnership units.

The assets of the partnership must be valued by a qualified business valuation expert to determine the value of the limited partnership interests. This valuation should be done before assets are transferred into the partnership. The purpose of the valuation is to substantiate the valuation discount that will be claimed on the gifted limited partnership units.

Who Should Consider Using a Family Limited Partnership?

The FLP should be considered by those who look to transfer assets to the next generation and yet desire to retain control of the assets gifted. The fact that the FLP shields the assets of the limited partners from creditors is also an advantage.

The following costs should also be taken into account: attorney's fees and accounting fees, the appraisal or valuation fee, updated appraisal fees each time partnership units are given as gifts, the Pennsylvania reality transfer tax (if real estate is transferred to the limited partnership), and the cost for the preparation of the partnership's annual income tax return (Form 1065).

Max's Family Limited Partnership

Max owns a commercial property valued at $110,000 and wants to make a gift to his daughter, Sue, which qualifies for the annual exclusion amount. Max could do this by conveying to Sue, by deed, a one-tenth interest in the property, which would equal $11,000. On the other hand, Max could transfer the property into an FLP and name himself the general partner. Thereafter, Max would own 2% of the partnership as a general partner, but maintain 100% control. He would also own the remaining 98% interest in the partnership as limited partner interests.

After establishing the FLP, Max could then make a gift of $11,000 worth of limited partnership units to Sue. This would be conveying greater than a one-tenth interest in the commercial property because the value of the limited partnership units is discounted. The value of the limited partnership interest is discounted for two reasons. One, because of the minority interest discount. This discount is based upon the fact that limited partners have no authority regarding the management of the partnership. The second discount is for the lack of marketability. This is based upon the fact that the limited partnership agreement restricts the transfer of the limited partnership interests. These two discounts together may result in a total discount of 20% to 40% of the value of the underlying assets.

The result of this discount is that assets can be transferred over a faster period of time to the next generation while parents maintain control during the entire process. For example, if parents were given a valuation by a qualified business valuation expert permitting a 30% discount for lack of marketability and control, they would be able to gift limited partnership units valued at $28,571. ($28,571 discounted by 30% = $19,999.70) Mother and Father would together be able to give this amount to each of their children. The net result of the discount is that the parents would be able to give away the entire asset in the limited partnership in a much shorter time period than if they were gifting the asset itself without the benefit of a limited partnership.

A Caution Regarding Pennsylvania Realty Transfer Tax

When using real estate to establish an FLP, Pennsylvania realty transfer tax will be due upon conveying by deed the real estate into the name of the FLP. This transfer tax is 2% of the assessed value of the real estate contributed, multiplied by the common level ratio as established for each county. The tax is higher in Alleghany and Philadelphia Counties.

Strategy Number Five: Prepay Estate Tax with Discounted Life Insurance Dollars

If there is still exposure to the federal estate tax after utilizing marital and charitable deductions, using both spouses' lifetime exclusion amounts, and removing as many assets as possible from your estate, the next strategy is to use life insurance to provide the liquidity necessary to pay the anticipated estate tax that will be due.

THE ROLE OF LIFE INSURANCE IN ESTATE PLANNING

Many are familiar with utilizing life insurance benefits to replace the income stream of a family wage earner upon death. When purchased for this purpose, the money spent on life insurance is often compared to money spent for fire insurance. It is an expense that only pays off if something bad happens — a fire or a death.

The use of life insurance in estate planning, however, is different. Life insurance has numerous unique tax benefits. With careful planning, life insurance can be a useful tool that can pass substantial assets to heirs, totally tax free.

Life insurance, because of its tax free benefits, is used in a variety of ways to achieve estate planning strategies.

Life Insurance as a Wealth Replacement Tool

When donors use charitable gifting techniques to favor their charities, the charitable deduction is permitted for assets transferred to qualified charities. The donor's children, however, may feel disinherited because a portion of their inheritance was given to charity. Life insurance can be used as an efficient method to replace the value of the gift given to charity. In addition, life insurance may be used to replace the value of the IRA that went to charity.

Using the Cash from Life Insurance to Pay Federal Estate Taxes

Often, stocks and bonds must be sold to pay the federal estate tax, and the timing of the sale can result in significant losses.

Life insurance is also used to provide liquidity to pay federal estate taxes. The fact that federal estate tax is due nine months after death sometimes requires a forced sale of assets to raise the cash needed to pay the tax. Often, stocks and bonds must be sold to raise the cash to pay the tax and the timing of the sale can result in significant losses based on the current price of the stock. If one has life insurance, there will be cash to pay the tax to avoid the forced sale of real estate, farm or business interest, or stocks.

Survivorship life insurance policies insure both spouses on one policy with a last-to-die provision. These policies can be purchased to pay the estate tax for lower premiums than individual policies on each spouse. This policy usually is more likely to be approved even if one spouse is in poor health, since the death benefit is not paid until the second spouse dies. These policies are sometimes referred to as second-to-die policies.

Buy-Sell Agreements Funded by Life Insurance

Life insurance is also used to fund business BUY-SELL AGREEMENTS. Partnerships and closely held businesses should have buy-sell agreements whereby at the death of one partner or shareholder, the surviving partners or shareholders must pay the estate of the deceased for the right to inherit his or her business interests. In order to avoid placing a heavy demand on the cash flow of the business, life insurance is used to fund these agreements to provide the cash necessary to buy out the share of the deceased business owner.

WHAT IS AN IRREVOCABLE LIFE INSURANCE TRUST?

Life insurance death benefits are exempt from federal income tax. What surprises many, however, is that life insurance death benefits can be included in the estate of the person who owned the policy. For example, if Father purchased a $500,000 life insurance policy on his life, and he is the owner, at his death the entire $500,000 would be included in his estate for federal estate tax purposes. For this reason, the IRREVOCABLE LIFE INSURANCE TRUST (ILIT) was developed to protect life insurance proceeds from the federal estate tax.

BENEFITS OF AN IRREVOCABLE LIFE INSURANCE TRUST

Tax Benefits

ILITs will reduce or eliminate federal estate taxes, thereby transferring a greater amount of inheritance to your heirs. This tax benefit is due to the fact that the life insurance in the ILIT is not owned by the taxpayer. Therefore, since the taxpayer does not own the policy, upon his or her death there is no federal estate tax on the death benefits.

Control Benefits

ILITs are used to ensure that life insurance benefits are not subject to the federal estate tax.

ILITs also provide control over the death benefit of life insurance, even after the insured's death. Typically, the beneficiary of life insurance receives the proceeds from the life insurance company immediately after the death of the insured. Beneficiaries have full control over the money as soon as they receive the proceeds. If the insured established an ILIT to receive the insurance benefits, on the other hand, the terms of the ILIT control the proceeds and pay out the distributions over time. One-half of the proceeds could be paid out on the death of the insured, for example, and the remaining one-half could be paid on the fifth annual anniversary of the death of the insured. This type of payout ensures that if the beneficiary squanders the first payout, he or she gets a second chance, five years later, to be a better steward of the money.

Liquidity Benefits

ILITs provide the cash necessary to pay federal estate taxes and other last expenses upon the death of the insured. In addition, life insurance is used in business succession planning to provide liquidity for children who are not involved in a family business, so they can receive an inheritance other than an interest in the family business.

Support for Surviving Spouse

ILITs can provide a lifetime of income and principal, if desired, for the surviving spouse. After the death of the surviving spouse, the balance of the ILIT can be distributed tax free to the heirs.

ILITs can be written to specify the amount and timing of the payout of life insurance benefits.

Leverage the Annual Exclusion Amount

In the section on gifting, we discussed the $11,000 annual exclusion amount that can be given as a gift to any number of people. Instead of giving $11,000 directly to children as a gift, however, there is an additional benefit to transferring the $11,000 into an ILIT for the benefit of the children. Once in the trust, the $11,000 could be used to pay the premium on life insurance on the grantor. The result is that the value of the annual exclusion amount has been maximized and has resulted in far greater value to the children after the death of the grantor.

How Life Insurance Trusts Are Established

To establish an ILIT, the grantor creates the ILIT and names a trustee to administer it. The grantor also names the beneficiaries of the ILIT to receive the proceeds upon the grantor's death (these are usually the same people named in his or her will or living trust). The grantor is *not* permitted to be the trustee of his or her own ILIT. Some people name their adult children trustee if they will also be the ultimate beneficiaries of the trust. Banks, trust companies or the grantor's CPA can also serve as trustee. The trustee is responsible to obtain the ILIT's taxpayer ID number from the IRS. This is necessary because the ILIT is considered a new taxpayer and is responsible to pay the tax on any income.

After the grantor creates the ILIT, the trustee is responsible to administer the trust during grantor's lifetime and distribute the ILIT assets to the beneficiaries after the grantor's death.

The trust must be established *before* the life insurance is purchased, so the trustee can sign the insurance application listing the trust as the applicant, owner and beneficiary of the policy, and the grantor as the insured. If the grantor were to own the policy first, and then transfer it into the trust, the three-year rule would apply. This rule states that if the grantor dies within three years of transferring an exisiting policy into the trust, the trust will be disregarded and the insurance proceeds become taxable for the estate tax.

> Once an ILIT is established, it cannot be amended or revoked, nor can funds placed in the trust be returned to the grantor. The trust is irrevocable. As a result, the IRS allows trust assets to be transferred tax free to heirs on the grantor's death.

Operation of an Irrevocable Life Insurance Trust

Once the ILIT has been designed, written and signed, the grantor funds the ILIT by giving money to the trustee. The trustee then signs the application for life insurance and makes the premium payments to the insurance company. It is important to confirm that the grantor *never has any ownership* of the life insurance. Therefore, after the grantor establishes the ILIT, every contribution the grantor makes must be to the trustee, and the trustee then pays the insurance premiums.

Each year the grantor can gift up to $11,000 to each trust beneficiary into the ILIT. This is the GIFT TAX annual exclusion amount. A husband and wife can gift a total of $22,000 per beneficiary of the ILIT each year.

After the trustee has received a contribution, the trustee must notify each beneficiary that a contribution has been made to the trust. The reason for this notice is that the gift must be a PRESENT INTEREST in order to qualify for the gift tax annual exclusion of up to $11,000 per year. Each contribution to the trust is considered a gift to the beneficiaries. Each beneficiary must be given reasonable notice (thirty days) to claim their portion of the gift. If a beneficiary does not claim his or her portion of the contribution, the trustee is then free to invest it wherever the trustee desires, which would be to pay insurance premiums. Since the long-term benefit of tax-free life insurance proceeds is more substantial than the short-term gift to the trust, a beneficiary may waive the right of withdrawal offered in the Crummey letter. After any beneficiaries decline to demand distribution of their proportionate share of the gift from the trust, the trustee then uses the gifted money to pay the life insurance premium.

One must be cautious when transferring *existing* life insurance policies into life insurance trusts. If the grantor dies within three years of the date of transferring an existing policy into a trust, the IRS will include the total death benefit in their taxable estate. Transferring existing policies into a life insurance trust may also trigger the gift tax.

The Bob & Shirley Jones Irrevocable Life Insurance Trust

Mr. and Mrs. Jones established the Bob and Shirley Jones Irrevocable Life Insurance Trust naming their son, Tim, the trustee. The contributions that the Joneses make to the ILIT are in the form of a check made out to Tim Jones, trustee of the Bob and Shirley Jones Irrevocable Life Insurance Trust. After the grantors give the check to the trustee, the trustee deposits the check into a non-interest-bearing checking account. Since the trust has its own taxpayer ID number, any interest earned is taxed to the trust. By using a non-interest bearing checking account, there is no taxable income and the trust can avoid the expense of filing tax returns.

What Happens When the Grantor Dies?

Upon the death of the grantor, the trustee collects the life insurance proceeds and distributes the ILIT assets as instructed in the trust document. The trustee must not directly pay the expenses or taxes due on the estate of the grantor. Although the trustee has access to this tax-free liquid fund to pay taxes and final expenses, if he or she used this money to pay the taxes or last expenses of the deceased grantor directly from the ILIT, then the entire amount in the ILIT would be taxed for federal estate tax purposes. Therefore, ILIT cash must be either loaned to the estate or used to purchase assets from the estate in order to use it to pay estate bills and taxes.

Tim and Jim Receive Crummey Letters

Mr. and Mrs. Jones named their two children, Tim and Jim, as the beneficiaries of their ILIT. Since Mr. and Mrs. Jones can each give $11,000 to each son, they can contribute a total amount of $44,000 to the insurance trust free of gift tax considerations. Once the $44,000 has been received by Tim, as trustee, he is required to send a letter to his brother. (Since Tim is the trustee he is deemed to have knowledge of the gift and is not required to receive notice of trust contributions.) The letter tells Jim that: (a) a $44,000 gift has been made to the trust; (b) Jim's proportionate share of the gift is $22,000; and, (c) Jim has thirty days within which to notify the trustee to distribute this amount to him. These letters of notification are called "Crummey letters." These letters are described in more detail in the preceding section on gifts to minors. (*See the Appendix for a sample Crummey letter.*)

"CAN'T I JUST HAVE MY CHILDREN OWN THE POLICY?"

After reviewing the requirements of ILITs, many people reach the conclusion that it would be simpler to have their children own the life insurance policy. If adult children own the policy, there is no requirement to go through the steps needed with ILITs. The life insurance will still be tax free at the death of the grantor because the grantor does not own the policy, the grantor's children do. Although it may appear simpler to have adult children own the life insurance, there are a number of risks to be considered:

- **Loss of control:** As owners of the policy, the children have the power to change the beneficiary. In addition, they would be free to either cancel the policy or withdraw all the cash value from the policy reducing the death benefit.
- **Your children may not use the death benefit as planned:** As owners of the policy, children receive all the proceeds directly from the insurance company. Your plan might be for them to use this money to pay last expenses and federal estate taxes, but

Rita and Henry Planned Well

Rita and Henry Babcock have died and now their estate needs $200,000 to pay federal estate taxes, inheritance taxes, deferred income taxes on annuities and IRAs and last expenses! Fortunately, the Babcocks benefited from careful estate planning with a knowledgeable team of professionals. They established an irrevocable life insurance trust funded with $200,000 in life insurance. If the trustee of the ILIT, their son Jack, uses that money to pay the federal estate taxes or last expenses directly, the entire amount of the ILIT would be subject to federal estate taxes. The ILIT, however, has a provision in it that permits the trustee to purchase assets from the estate. If the Babcock's owned a home worth $200,000 for example, it would be permissible for the trustee to transfer $200,000 in cash to the estate and in return receive the decedents' home valued at $200,000. After this transaction, there is $200,000 in cash in the estate, and the estate can use that money to pay last expenses and taxes. The terms of the trust state that after the death of both grantors whatever is left in the trust is to be distributed equally to their children.

there is no requirement for them to do so. They may use the life insurance proceeds to do as they please. In addition, the parents would be giving the money to pay the insurance premiums directly to their children and hope that the children would then use it to pay the insurance premiums.

Although it may appear simpler to have adult children own the life insurance, there are a number of risks.

- **The policy would be subject to the children's creditors:** The cash value of the policy is available to the creditors of each child in the event of their bankruptcy, a business failure, high medical bills or a divorce.
- **If son or daughter dies first, their surviving spouse would own the policy:** If the surviving son-in-law or daughter-in-law should remarry, the new husband or wife would be an owner. The cash value is included in the estate of the child if he or she dies before the parents.

- **Administrative difficulties:** If the policy is owned jointly by children, then all the children must sign all necessary forms.

TRUST PROTECTOR POWERS

In light of the possible repeal of the federal estate tax, making a trust irrevocable could be troubling to some. It is true that the future of the estate tax is uncertain. It will bring us an increasing lifetime exclusion amount and a decreasing estate tax rate. We also have the possibility of a complete repeal of the estate tax in 2010 and its subsequent reinstatement the following year. During this period of uncertainty, the key word regarding estate planning is *flexibility*. Yet, irrevocable life insurance trusts continue to have their place as an estate planning strategy. In order to enhance their flexibility, however, many estate planners are writing into irrevocable life insurance trusts a trust protector provision.

ILITs can be written with provisions to enhance their flexibility in light of possible changes in federal estate tax laws.

Trust protectors can be given the authority to change the terms of the trust in the event that the taxpayer's situation or tax laws change. It is possible to allow changes to the trust to be made in the event that the estate tax is repealed or the value of the grantor's estate falls below the current lifetime exclusion amount.

Choosing the individual or institution to serve as trust protector can be a challenge. Due to the wide scope of changes that can be permitted (even including changing beneficial interest) a beneficiary should *not* be named a trust protector. A trust protector may be given the authority to modify or amend the terms of the trust in order to achieve certain tax advantages. Their authority to amend the trust can be so broad as to be any reason that the trust protector believes to be necessary or desirable. The trust protector could also be given the authority to terminate the trust and distribute all trust assets to the beneficiaries; the ability to do so would have to be specified in the trust. Of course, the trust protector should be restricted from making any modification or change that would significantly change any beneficiary's interest under the trust.

DISADVANTAGES OF IRREVOCABLE LIFE INSURANCE TRUSTS

There are two *dis*advantages to irrevocable life insurance trusts:

A beneficiary should not be named a trust protector because trust protectors can modify the terms of the trust.

1. ILITs cannot be amended or revoked once established. The grantor can stop making the contributions that the trustee was using to pay premiums, but that does not terminate the ILIT. The ILIT would continue to own the remaining cash value in the life insurance policy.
2. The grantor loses the use of the money contributed. In addition, the grantor will not have access to any growth in the cash value.
3. If the federal estate tax is repealed, and the ILIT was established for the sole purpose of avoiding the federal estate tax, the grantor may not want to have a high cash value locked up in the ILIT.

WHO SHOULD CONSIDER USING AN IRREVOCABLE LIFE INSURANCE TRUST?

Those who have significant estate tax exposure should give these trusts serious consideration. In addition, those who wish to have continued control over the disposition of life insurance benefits even after their death should consider an ILIT.

Summary

Although the federal estate tax has a rate as high as 50% on estates over $1 million dollars (in 2002), we have seen five fundamental strategies that can be used to minimize the effects of this tax. More planning opportunities are available to those who are married, although single taxpayers have a number of planning strategies as well.

Irrevocable Life Insurance Trust Procedures

Task	To Be Completed By	Required Completion Date
Design and write trust	Attorney	Before life insurance application is signed
Obtain tax ID number from the IRS	Attorney	When trust is written
Sign trust agreement	Trustee and Grantors	
Prepare application for life insurance	Insurance agent	After trust is written and signed
Trustee signs application as owner and names trust the beneficiary	Trustee	After trust and life insurance applications are completed
Open a non-interest bearing checking account in trust's tax ID number to deposit trust contributions and pay insurance premiums	Trustee	Immediately after signing trust
Grantor makes check out to trustee	Grantor	
Trustee endorses all checks and deposits them into trust checking account	Trustee	
Send Crummey withdrawal notices to beneficiaries	Trustee	As soon as funds are contributed to trust
Pay the insurance premium after the withdrawal period has passed by writing checks to the insurance company out of the trust checking account	Trustee	After Crummey withdrawal period has passed
Contribute additional funds to trust to pay premium in future years	Grantor	At least 30 days before premium is due
Upon death of insureds, distribution of trust assets	Trustee	According to the terms of the trust

Part V

What Will You Leave Behind of Lasting Significance?

"We make a living by what we get. We make a life by what we give."

– Winston Churchill

10

Charitable Estate Planning

Topics Include

Qualifications of Charitable Gifts & Charities
Popular Giving Tools
Gifts that Give Back
Charitable Remainder Trusts
Wealth Replacement Trusts
Charitable Lead Trusts
Pooled Income Funds
Remainder Interests
Conservation Easements
Foundations
Donor-Advised Funds
Charitable Estate Planning with IRAs & Qualified Retirement Plans

Introduction

According to "Giving USA: The annual report on philanthropy," Americans gave $203.5 billion to charities in 2000. Lifetime gifts by individuals totaled approximately $152 billion of this amount, or about 75% of total giving. Gifts by wills represented about 8% of total giving at $16 billion. Religious organizations received 36% of all contributions, and educational organizations received 14% of all contributions.

Over the next thirty-five years as much as $41 trillion will be transferred from the parents of baby boomers to their children.

Some researchers predict that over the next thirty-five years as much as $41 *trillion* will be transferred from the parents of baby boomers to their children. Charitable giving will play an immense role in this transfer of wealth. Although charitable estate planning provides many personal and tax benefits, it has a more fundamental benefit. Taxes collected from estates are in a sense "involuntary charitable giving," with the decedent never knowing how the tax collected was spent. Charitable estate planning, on the other hand, is voluntary charitable giving. With proper planning, individuals can direct money from their estate *to be paid to those programs they desire.* This chapter provides a broad framework within which to consider charitable gifts.

What Is Charitable Estate Planning?

The motivations for making charitable gifts are as numerous as the people making them. Gifts are given to hospitals, cancer funds and heart associations in memory of loved ones who have died from health challenges. Gifts are also given to colleges and universities with a view toward helping the disadvantaged receive the quality education that the donor received. Whether the motivation is based on religious conviction, a long-term relationship with a charity, or a desire to leverage the tax benefits, charitable estate planning is full of opportunities and emerging possibilities to increase and maximize gift assets. In addition, many families are beginning to realize that transferring the values of the senior generation to the younger generation is equally as important as getting a tax benefit. Using charitable estate planning to transfer both one's values and one's assets to the next generation is unlimited.

What Is a Charitable Gift?

A gift must meet three tests in order for the IRS to permit a tax deduction to the donor. First, the donor must give up all control of the gift, there can be no strings attached to the gift. Second, the donor must deliver the gift to a qualified charity. Lastly, the charity must accept the gift and provide no benefit back to the donor.

WHAT IS A QUALIFIED CHARITY?

Charitable gifts must be made to a qualified charity in order to be income tax deductible. A qualified charity is one that is a charitable organization as described in Internal Revenue Code §501(c)(3). Such organizations will be referred to throughout this chapter as charities.

All non-profit organizations are defined by the IRS as either "public charities" or "private foundations." Public charities are churches, schools, hospitals and medical research organizations, for example. All public charities rely on public support. Private foundations, on the other hand, are usually funded by an individual or corporation and receive no support from the public. The main difference to the donor as to whether a charity is a public charity or a private foundation is the amount of income tax deductions permitted for contributions to the charity.

Income tax deduction benefits apply only to charities that are described in Internal Revenue Code §501(c)(3).

It is important to confirm that the organization you are contributing to is a qualified charitable organization. The IRS provides a list of qualified charities in IRS Publication 78 *Cumulation List of Organizations Described In §170(c) of the Internal Revenue Code.* This publication should not be relied upon as the sole source of information concerning qualified charities as names are constantly being added and deleted. Upon request, most charities will send you a copy of their IRS tax-exempt letter.

TAX BENEFITS & LIMITATIONS OF CHARITABLE GIFTS

The IRS permits income tax benefits for those who itemize their tax deductions on their tax return. There are limits, however, on the deductions permitted.

The income tax deduction limits are based on the type of organization that the donor is contributing to as well as the type of assets that make up the gift. The maximum allowable deduction for charitable contributions of cash to public charities is 50% of the donor's "contribution base," which is essentially the same as the donor's adjusted gross income. Cash contributions to private foundations, on the other hand, are limited to only 30% of the donor's contribution base.

Long-term capital gain assets (held by the donor for longer than one year) that is contributed to public charities is deductible only to the extent of 30% of the donor's contribution base. The contribution to a private foundation of the same type of assets is limited to 20% of the donor's contribution base. If contributions exceed any of these limits, the tax deduction may be carried forward for up to five succeeding tax years.

> It is important to note that these percentage limits are for income tax deductions only. Gifts made to charities receive a 100% charitable deduction from the estate and gift tax.

THE RULES OF VALUATION

The amount of the charitable deduction allowed for gifts is based upon the fair market value of the donated assets. Fair market value is defined by the IRS as the price at which the assets change hands between a willing buyer and a willing seller, both having a reasonable knowledge of all relevant facts. That may be easier said than done and the IRS has specific rules and guidelines for determining the value of gifts. These rules cover such assets as listed securities, mutual funds, life insurance, closely-held stock, real estate, personal property and works of art. In order to receive a deduction for the gift, it is important to comply with the valuation requirements of the IRS. Most public charities are familiar with the reporting requirements and will explain those affecting your gift.

Popular Giving Tools

DIRECT GIFTS TO CHARITIES

Direct gifts to charities are the simplest form of gift and result in an income tax deduction in the year that the gift is made. Direct gifts can be made in the form of cash, listed securities, mutual funds, bonds, personal property, life insurance policies or real estate. This type of gift is used by those who want their gifts to immediately assist the charity. It is better to donate appreciated assets directly to the charity instead of selling the assets and donating the cash. This way, no one pays the capital gains tax on the sale of the appreciated asset.

It is better to donate appreciated assets to the charity instead of selling the assets and donating the cash.

CHARITABLE BEQUESTS

There are several ways to make gifts through wills or living trusts:

1. The donor specifies a dollar amount. For example, "$5,000 to my church."
2. A donor gives specific assets to charity such as "my hunting cabin or shore property" or specific stocks or bonds.
3. The donor gives a percentage of the total estate to charity. For example, "10% of the value of my estate to the Boys & Girls Club."
4. The donor specifies that the residual estate goes to one or more charities. This would be the case if one desired to gift what is left of the estate after taxes and expenses to charity.

BARGAIN SALE

A BARGAIN SALE occurs when the donor sells assets to a charity for an amount *less than* the assets' fair market value. If such a sale were made to a non-qualified charity (such as the donor's child), the difference between the fair market value and the payment received by the seller is treated as a gift to the buyer. The IRS treats that transaction as part sale/part gift.

When the bargain sale is made to a qualified charity, however, the difference between the fair market value and the payment received by the donor is a tax deductable charitable contribution to the charity. Real estate is a common asset sold to charities as a bargain sale, although any asset would qualify. Bargain sales offer flexibility with regard to gifts to charities by providing the donor with some cash from the sale of the assets to charity. Bargain sales do not avoid all of the capital gains tax on appreciated assets. There will be capital gains tax due on the portion of the sales proceeds that the donor keeps although the income tax deduction may offset the tax effect of the gain. The fair market value must be substantiated by a qualified appraiser.

> It is very important that the bequest language include the exact legal name of the charity and its complete address. In addition, the bequest language may include any specific purposes for the gift or restrictions on its use.

The Gift of an Undivided Portion of a Donor's Interest in Assets

Transferring to charity only a portion of the donor's total interest in some assets qualifies as a gift. This strategy permits the donor to sell his or her assets at the highest and best price, yet have a portion of the sales price paid to the charity, since the charity will own a portion of the assets sold.

The gift of a partial interest in assets commonly occurs when the donor is planning to sell highly appreciated real estate. For example, a donor may give a charity an undivided one-third interest as tenant in common in a farm or commercial property. The donor receives an immediate income tax deduction based upon the value of the one-third interest. When the real estate is sold, the donor receives two-thirds of the sales proceeds and the charity receives the other one-third. With this strategy, the capital gains tax on the proceeds from the sale of the portion of the property kept can be offset by the charitable deduction provided by the gift to charity before the sale.

The Deferred Charitable Gift Annuity

For those who would like to make a tax deductable gift now and receive income later, the deferred charitable gift annuity is an option. When establishing a deferred charitable gift annuity, the donor makes a gift to the charity and the charity agrees to pay a guaranteed fixed income for life, which will not begin until a date in the future. Although the payments do not start until the future date, the donor receives the charitable income tax deduction in the year of the gift.

Gifts That Give Back

CHARITABLE GIFT ANNUITIES

A charitable gift annuity is appropriate for those who wish to give to charity but have a need for income from their gift. It is a contractual agreement wherein the donor *irrevocably* transfers cash, securities or real estate to the charity. In exchange, the charity pays to the donor (and another beneficiary if the donor chooses) for the donor's lifetime, a guaranteed fixed income. The charitable gift annuity is part charitable gift and part an annuity investment. The amount paid for charitable gift annuities will exceed that required to be paid to a commercial insurance company to receive the same annuity income. The amount in excess of the commercial value of the annuity reflects the donor's intent to make a charitable contribution. The annuity payments must be made at least annually and can begin at a date later than the date of the gift.

The donor receives an immediate income tax deduction of up to 50% of the donor's contribution base in the year in which the annuity is acquired. Any deduction not permitted to be taken in the year of acquisition can be carried forward for an additional five years. The amount of the deduction is based upon the amount of the contribution, the age of the donor and the payment frequency.

A charitable gift annuity is perhaps the most popular life income gift.

A portion of each annuity payment received by the donor is tax free until the donor reaches his or her IRS-determined life expectancy. After reaching that age, payments received are fully taxable as ordinary income. The age of the donor at the time the annuity is established determines the amount of the annuity payment. Most charities use the rate schedule suggested by the American Council on Gift Annuities.

In addition to the tax benefits, another advantage to charitable gift annuities is the elimination of the estate tax on the assets used to purchase the charitable gift annuity. In addition, in contrast with a number of other charitable planning strategies, there are no legal or accounting fees required to establish a charitable gift annuity.

There is an advantage to acquiring charitable gift annuities using appreciated stock or real estate. If the appreciated stock or real estate were sold, capital gains tax would have to be paid on the appreciation. If, on the other hand, the appreciated asset was transferred to a charity in exchange for a charitable gift annuity, capital gains tax is reduced. This is because part of the capital gains is allocated to the donated portion of the asset and is extinguished. The balance of capital gains is not all reportable in the year of the gift (as it would be if the donor had sold the securities or real estate). To the contrary, the gain is only reported as it is received over the annuitant's lifetime. The donor is entitled to a charitable contribution deduction equal to the excess in value between the fair market value of the assets transferred to the charity and the value of the annuity.

Charitable Remainder Trust

A CHARITABLE REMAINDER TRUST is a trust which permits a donor to convert appreciated assets (for example, stocks or real estate) into increased lifetime income while paying no capital gains tax when the asset is sold. Of course, the donor can also use cash to fund a charitable trust.

BENEFITS OF CHARITABLE REMAINDER TRUSTS

Consider making the gift using a charitable remainder trust during your lifetime to achieve a current income tax deduction.

Charitable remainder trusts permit a gift to charity while reserving an income stream to you for the rest of your life. Income taxes are reduced due to the charitable income tax deduction allowed for contributions to the trust. If you intend to make a charitable gift after death, consider making the gift now using a charitable remainder trust to achieve the added benefit of a current income tax deduction. Estate taxes are also reduced because the asset is removed from your taxable estate.

These trusts also allow you to convert highly appreciated assets into other investments that may return a higher yield and avoid paying capital gains tax in the process.

HOW CHARITABLE TRUSTS ARE ESTABLISHED

The donor funds the charitable remainder trust by transferring assets to it. This is done by re-registering the assets (real estate or other assets) into the name of the trustee of the trust. If the trust is being funded with real estate, a deed is prepared conveying the real estate into the name of the trustee of the trust. When real estate or other hard-to-value assets are contributed to a charitable remainder trust, an appraisal is required by a qualified appraiser to confirm the fair market value of the assets contributed. If stocks, bonds or mutual fund shares are placed into the trust, the account name of the stocks would be re-registered into the name of the trustee.

When real estate or other hard-to-value assets are contributed to a charitable remainder trust an appraisal is required.

The trustee then makes payments to the donor (and/or other income beneficiaries) for the rest of his life, or for a specific term of years up to twenty years.

The trustee may sell the assets at fair market value and reinvest the sales proceeds. Since the charitable remainder trust is a tax-free entity, it does not incur a capital gains tax on any revenue realized by the sale of the appreciated assets transferred into the trust.

Trust payments may be made to the donor alone or to both the donor and the donor's spouse, so long as either is living. Another strategy is to make the payment to the donor's children. At the death of the survivor of all beneficiaries, or after a term of years selected by the donor, the trust ends and the trustee transfers the trust assets to one or more charities named in the trust. This ultimate transfer to the charity is what generates the tax benefits.

Although charitable remainder trusts are irrevocable, the donor may retain some control. For example, the donor is permitted to serve as trustee of the trust, thereby making all investment management decisions. In addition, the donor may retain the right to change the trustee of the trust or change the charity or charities that receive the balance of the trust after the death of the beneficiaries. Since this change can even be made in the donor's will, he will always have control over which charities will ultimately receive the balance of the trust. The donor may also make additional contributions to a charitable remainder unitrust. If the donor established a charitable remainder annuity trust, however, no additional contributions are permitted (*discussed on page 203*).

Choosing the Trustee

The donor is permitted to serve as trustee of his charitable trust. When doing so, it is important to name a successor trustee in case the donor would no longer be able or willing to serve as trustee. The charity can also serve as trustee. When the charity is involved in the planning process, this arrangement makes sense. Charities may or may not charge for this service. A bank or trust company trustees may also be named. The trustee will be responsible for managing the investments, keeping all records, filing tax returns and making distributions to the beneficiaries. (*Please review Chapter 5 for a complete discussion on trustee duties.*)

The charity can also serve as trustee. When the charity is involved in the planning process, this arrangement makes sense.

Choosing Trust Assets

Appreciated stock or real estate provides the greatest tax benefits when used to fund a charitable trust. This is due to the fact that the trust is not required to pay capital gains tax when it sells the assets. Therefore, the lower the basis of the contributed assets, the more capital gains tax savings is available. Real estate, stocks and bonds are all good candidates to fund the trust. There can be no written agreement for sale requiring the trust to sell real estate before it is contributed to the trust. Also, the existence of a mortgage on real estate will cause unwanted tax results.

FIXED PAYOUT (CHARITABLE REMAINDER ANNUITY TRUST)

There are two choices on how you can receive your payments from a charitable remainder trust. The amount of the trust's payment to the income recipient does not fluctuate under the CHARITABLE REMAINDER ANNUITY TRUST (CRAT). When the trust is established, you choose the percentage payout rate desired. The higher the payment, the lower your charitable deduction. The specified sum paid annually may not be less than 5% and not more than 50% of the fair market value of all assets used to fund the trust. The highest allowable payout rate is based on your age and current interest rates. For example, in late 2001 a fifty-year-old donor would have a maximum payout of 8% and a sixty-five-year-old donor would have 10%. The payment is fixed when the trust is established and does not fluctuate. Another example would be if you were to place $100,000 into a charitable remainder annuity trust and establish the payout percentage to yourself at 6%, you would receive $6,000 per year, every year, regardless of the investment performance of the $100,000 (6% of $100,000 is $6,000). The value of the trust may fluctuate even if your payment does not. This type of payout may be preferred by older clients who desire a fixed payout amount. (A disadvantage to this approach is that more assets cannot be added to a charitable remainder annuity trust once it is established, and if inflation increases, the fixed payment will have less purchasing power.)

When the trust is established, you choose the payout rate. The higher the payment, the lower your charitable deduction.

VARIABLE PAYOUT (CHARITABLE REMAINDER UNITRUST, 3 TYPES)

When a CHARITABLE REMAINDER UNITRUST (CRUT) is established, you choose the percentage payout rate that you wish just as you would with a CRAT. The difference is that a CRUT must have its assets revalued every year and the chosen payout rate is multiplied times this annual value to determine the trust's payment for that year. The CRUT pays a fixed percentage of the trust assets that may not be less than 5% and not more than 50% of the fair market value of the trust assets as determined every year. At the time the trust is initially funded, the percentage payout rate is multiplied by the value of the trust assets to determine the payment you will receive for that year only. The payment in future years will fluctuate based on the investment performance as reflected in the annual value of the trust. The trust is revalued on the same date each year, and each year's income paid out is determined by multiplying the chosen percentage payout rate times the value of the trust.

> If you established your CRUT in 2002 with $100,000 and chose a 6% payout rate, your income for the year 2002 would be $6,000. However, if on January 1, 2003, the trust value was $110,000, your income for 2003 would be $6,600 ($110,000 x 6%). Although the percent is fixed, the income received may increase or decrease over time as the trust assets grow or shrink. Standard unitrust rules require that if not enough interest and dividends are earned by the CRUT to provide the amount required to be distributed, any shortfall must be made up by invading the principal of the CRUT.

A variation of the charitable remainder unitrust is the net income with makeup charitable remainder unitrust (NIMCRUT). This type of trust makes payments of the *lesser* of the percentage payout rate established when the trust was funded, or the actual interest and dividends generated by the trust. This protects the principal from being invaded to make required payments. In our example above, if the trust required a payment of $6,000, but only generated $5,000 in interest and dividends, only $5,000 would be distributed. The advantage of this type of trust is that it avoids having to consume principal in order to make the payments. The makeup provision means that if the trust beneficiary is underpaid in years that the interest and dividends generated are not enough to make the payment required, the shortfall in payments may be made up in later years. This shortfall is made up when future amounts of interest and dividends generated by the trust are sufficient to not only make the current year's payments, but also make up for the unpaid payments from prior years.

A NIMCRUT protects the principal from being invaded to make required payments.

A third type of charitable remainder unitrust is known as a flip trust. A flip trust is a NIMCRUT that switches to a standard unitrust upon the occurrence of a designated event. The IRS allows charitable remainder trusts to flip from a NIMCRUT to a standard unitrust if the date or event triggering the conversion is beyond the control of the trustee or any other person. Permissible triggering events include marriage, divorce, death or birth of a child. A flip trust is used when a NIMCRUT is funded with non-income producing real estate. The trust can be established to "flip" into a standard unitrust upon the sale of the real estate that is in the charitable trust. NIMCRUT provisions are preferred during the period of time between funding the trust with the real estate and selling the real estate. This is because the trust has no income and the principal will not be required to be invaded to make required payouts. Once the real estate in the trust is sold, the standard trust would be preferred because the proceeds from the sale of the real estate would be invested to generate income and/or dividends from which to make the required payments.

TAX TREATMENT OF CHARITABLE TRUSTS

When a donor transfers assets into a charitable remainder trust, the donor receives a charitable income tax deduction.

Factors that determine the income tax deduction for contributions to a charitable trust:

1. ***Payout rate***
2. ***Value of assets***
3. ***Age and number of beneficiaries***
4. ***Frequency of payments***

The income tax deduction for contributions of appreciated assets to the trust is limited to 30% of the donor's contribution base. If the donor funds the trust with cash, the deduction increases to a limit of 50% of the donor's contribution base. The amount of deduction not taken in any one year can be carried forward for the subsequent five years unless exhausted sooner.

The amount of the income tax deduction is based on the value of the assets remaining in the trust at the time the charity receives them. The more the charity gets, the more deduction you get. The IRS uses a number of factors to calculate the income tax deduction allowed. The first is the pay-out rate established by the donor. The higher the pay-out percentage, the lower the income tax deduction. Another factor upon which the amount of the tax deduction depends is the value of the assets transferred into the trust. A third factor is the age and number of beneficiaries. The fewer and older the beneficiaries, the higher the income tax deduction. Lastly, the frequency of the payments (monthly vs. annual for example) has an impact on the value of the tax deduction.

The income tax that the donor pays on payments received from the charitable trust depends on the type of income the trust earned during each year. Charitable trusts are unique in that the beneficiaries' payments are taxed under a FOUR-TIER TAX TREATMENT. The four tiers are as follows: First, income received by the donor is taxed as ordinary income to the extent that the trust had ordinary income for the year (and any ordinary income from prior years that had not yet been distributed). The second tier is capital gains payments. If the trust did not generate enough ordinary income during the year to make the required distribution, capital gains are used to the extent that the trust had capital gains for the year and any undistributed capital gains from prior years. Third, payments received by the beneficiary will be taxed as tax-exempt income to the extent that the trust had tax-exempt income for the year. Lastly, distributions from the trust will be received as tax-free distributions of principal.

> Several years ago Harvey established his charitable remainder unitrust. It is a standard unitrust, and this year the trust has a required payout of $6,000, which Harvey receives. How Harvey reports the $6,000 tax on his income tax return depends upon the nature of the payment distributed by the trust. If the trust had only $2,000 of ordinary income for the year, and had no undistributed ordinary income from prior years, then $2,000 of the $6,000 would be taxed to Harvey as ordinary income. In addition to the ordinary income, if the trust had capital gains of another $3,000 during the year, then $3,000 of his $6,000 would be taxed as capital gains income. If the trustee had invested in some tax-free municipal bonds and those bonds earned income of $500, then the $500 received by Harvey would be received as tax-exempt income. The final $500 received by Harvey would be considered a tax-free distribution of principal if the trust did not earn enough from ordinary income, capital gains, or tax exempt income to generate the $6,000 necessary to distribute to Harvey.

WHO SHOULD CONSIDER USING CHARITABLE REMAINDER TRUSTS?

Those with charitable intent looking for an immediate income tax deduction and wishing to increase their current income should consider a charitable remainder trust. Also, those who own appreciated assets and have been reluctant to sell them because of the capital gains tax liability that would result would benefit from charitable trusts. By using the charitable remainder trust, assets could be sold, while avoiding any capital gains tax.

REPLACING CHARITABLE TRUST ASSETS WITH A WEALTH REPLACEMENT TRUST

A common concern when the charitable remainder trust is used for charitable estate planning is that the assets used to fund the trust are ultimately paid to charity. Therefore, the trust assets will not be available for the donor's family after the donor's death. Wealth replacement trusts are a common strategy to address this concern. The increased income provided to the donor from the charitable remainder trust, can be used to pay the premium on a life insurance policy that is structured to replace the value of the asset that was given to charity. Each year, money will be paid into an irrevocable life insurance trust to pay the premium on the life insurance used to replace the value of the asset for children upon the donor's death.

By using an irrevocable life insurance trust, the life insurance proceeds will be kept out of the donor's taxable estate. (*For a more detailed discussion on the use of life insurance trusts, please review Chapter 9.*)

Charitable Lead Trusts

A charitable lead trust permits the donor to pass assets in the future at a discounted value.

The CHARITABLE LEAD TRUST is the reverse of the charitable remainder trust. While the charitable remainder trust pays income to the donor for life, and pays the remainder to charity at the donor's death, the charitable lead trust pays income first to the charity for a term of years, and the remainder is *paid back* to the donor or intended beneficiaries. This means that the charity leads the interest of the non-charitable recipient.

The advantages to the donor of a charitable lead trust are that it permits the donor to pass assets to heirs and family in the future at a discounted value. The donor may also receive a tax deduction for the charities' interest.

The disadvantages of this trust include the fact that the income of the trust is taxed to the donor. In addition, the transfer of assets to the trust is irrevocable and the income tax deduction is limited.

Charitable lead trusts can be established either during one's lifetime or after death. The trust helps those who own income-producing assets and do not need the income. It would also be indicated if one desired to divert income to a charity for a specific period of time, but also desired to ultimately transfer the asset producing the income to a family member incurring no federal estate tax.

Pooled Income Funds

Many larger charities offer an alternative to the charitable remainder trust in the form of a pooled income fund. The pooled income fund is an entity that is established and administered by the charity, at no cost to the donor. The IRS treats a pooled income fund as an irrevocable trust that holds assets gifted by the charity's donors. All income received by the fund is distributed to the donor and is taxed as ordinary income. The trust makes income distributions to the donors for their lifetime, and upon their death the investments remaining in the pooled income fund are distributed only to the charity that sponsors the pooled income fund.

Pooled income funds have been described as mutual funds for charitable giving.

When making contributions to a pooled income fund, the donor pays no legal or accounting fees. The donor to the pooled income fund can also contribute highly appreciated assets and not pay capital gains tax. In addition, the donor receives a current income tax deduction for the present value of the remainder interest of the gift. The pooled income fund, however, has a disadvantage in that it is impossible to know the amount of income the donor will receive from year to year. Another disadvantage is the donor has no input into the investment decisions of the fund.

Remainder Interest in a Home or Farm

Normally, in order for a gift to be deductible for income tax purposes, the donor must donate to charity all of his rights to the assets. One exception to this rule that does qualify for an income tax deduction is the gift of a remainder interest in the donor's home, vacation property or farm. When making a gift of a remainder interest to charity, the donor will convey by deed his home, vacation property or farm to the charity, but will reserve the right to continue living there until death. The amount of the income tax deduction is equal to the value of the property at the time of death of the person granting the remainder interest. The gift of the remainder interest in a home need not be the entire interest, but could be a portion of the acreage: for example, only two acres out of a ten-acre tract of land, if that is what consists of the donor's home. The gift of the remainder interest for a farm also need not be the entire farm acreage, but may be any portion of the total acreage used as a farm.

Conservation Easements

The IRS permits an income tax deduction for the contribution of a qualified real property interest to a qualified organization so long as it is used exclusively for conservation purposes. One asset interest for which the IRS allows this tax deduction is a perpetual restriction on the use of land, known as a CONSERVATION EASEMENT. The conservation easement enables the donor to receive an income tax deduction for preserving his land in its existing state. The most significant benefit to the landowner, however, may not be tax related. The landowner will have the peace of mind that his land will remain as he has left it.

A conservation easement places restrictions on the use and future development of land.

A conservation easement places restrictions on the use and future development of land. The terms of the easement are written in an easement agreement that is recorded in the recorder of deeds office in the county in which the land is located. The easement describes the limits placed on the use of the land by the current and any future landowner. The easement is a perpetual restriction on the use of the land.

The restrictions that qualify as conservation easements include using land only for outdoor recreation or for preserving open space as forest or farmland pursuant to a government conservation policy. Historically important land areas and certified historic structures also qualify. The conservation easement must be granted to a qualified organization such as a local government or a publicly supported charity.

Conservation easements include using land only for outdoor recreation or for preserving open space as forest or farmland.

The donor receives a charitable deduction based upon the value of the development rights that the donor gave up in the conservation easement. The valuation process includes determining the value of the land without the easement and subtracting from that amount the value of the land after the easement is granted. These values must be determined by a qualified appraiser. There are no specified limits on use that are required for all conservation easements. One donor may choose to restrict all possible commercial development on his farm, while his neighbor might permit limited subdivision. The more subdivision or development that the donor permits, the lower the value of the easement, which results in a lower income tax deduction.

The organizations qualified to receive conservation easements are either government bodies or public charities known as land trusts. Officials of the land trust (or the government agency) will inspect the property periodically over the years to confirm that it is being used in compliance with the terms of the conservation easement.

The value of the conservation easement permitted as a federal income tax deduction is limited to 30% of the donor's contribution base. Any income tax deduction not taken in the year of the gift can be carried forward for an additional five years.

An additional tax advantage of conservation easements is that upon the donor's death, the value of the land with the easement will be much lower for purposes of the federal estate tax and the Pennsylvania inheritance tax.

Pennsylvania is the nation's leader in farmland preservation. Since 1989, Pennsylvania has protected more than 1,500 farms totaling more than 180,000 acres. In the year 2000 alone, 311 farms were preserved for a total of 33,270 acres. In 1999, the Legislature approved the "Growing Greener" legislation. Under this legislation, a total of $100,000,000 is earmarked for farmland preservation over a five-year period.

The Pennsylvania Department of Agriculture makes matching grants to counties that qualify. In the year 2000, $45 million was provided by the Pennsylvania Department of Agriculture which was matched by county funding to the extent of $24 million.

There are a number of factors that land must comply with to be eligible for the easement purchase program. First, the land must be enrolled in what is known as an agricultural security area. In addition, easements must be purchased on farms of a minimum of fifty acres in size (smaller parcels qualify if they are adjacent to existing preserved farmland). Other factors are considered such as the proximity of the farm to public water and sewer, and the extent of commercial development near the farm.

Those desiring more information on this program should contact the Bureau of Farmland Preservation, Pennsylvania Department of Agriculture, 2301 North Cameron Street, Harrisburg, Pennsylvania 17110-9408. Phone 717-783-3167.

Foundations

PRIVATE FOUNDATIONS

A private foundation is essentially a private tax-exempt organization whose purpose is to benefit charities, educational institutions, or other non-profit organizations of the donor's choosing. As a charitable organization, contributions to a private foundation qualify for tax deductions. Tax deduction limits for gifts to a private foundation are more restrictive than for gifts to a public charity. Gifts of cash to a private foundation may be deducted only up to 30% of the donor's contribution base. Gifts of appreciated assets may only be deducted up to 20% of the donor's contribution base. For a public charity, these limits are 50% for cash contributions and 30% for appreciated assets. For both types of charities, any excess deductions may be carried forward for five years.

Private foundations do not provide charitable services, but make grants to provide funding to qualified charities. Individuals and corporations have established more than 50,000 private foundations. It is created and controlled by a single source of funds (usually one individual or family) and not the general public. Private foundations are established to provide a greater degree of control to the donor, or his or her family, than is possible for public charities. The donor retains substantial control over administration and investment of the assets donated to the private foundation. Another reason that donors use private foundations is that they are excellent vehicles to transfer the donor's values to the next generation. This is accomplished by involving the younger generation in the administration and management of the foundation and its grants.

Private foundations are usually most appropriate for large contributions. Some writers suggest a minimum amount of $250,000.

Another advantage of private foundations is that the tax deduction is taken in the year of donations, but the amount contributed can be distributed to charities over the course of many years.

The governing form of a private foundation can be either a trust or a non-profit corporation. Once the organization has been established and the board of directors or trustees appointed, the IRS requires additional documentation. Private foundations must generally distribute at least 5% of their net investment assets to qualified charities each year. Establishing a foundation and complying with its reporting requirements incurs ongoing legal and accounting expenses.

Private foundations are appropriate for those who want control over the investment of the donated assets, as well as involvement in the making of grants for charitable purposes. They also provide the donor with recognition and publicity. Donors who establish private foundations can use them to channel all of the charitable giving of all family members into one vehicle. This would result in larger gifts for greater impact on charities.

Community Foundations

Community foundations are classified by the IRS as public charities. They are organized as a permanent collection of endowed funds for the long-term benefit of a defined geographic area. Establishing a fund or account at a community foundation achieves many of the same charitable objectives as a private foundation, but is far less costly to administer.

There are a number of advantages to community foundations. Contributors may deduct contributions up to 50% of their contribution base. Another advantage is that the donor's fund is exempt from filing its own tax return since its financial transactions are consolidated with those of other funds on the community foundation's tax return. These advantages, in addition to the wide latitude in choices in the naming of endowed funds, make the community foundation a popular choice for many donors.

The governing body of a community foundation is made up of representatives of the general public. Like private foundations, they operate primarily as grant-making organizations. Grants are made from each fund of a community foundation in accordance with the instructions the donor gave to the community foundation when he established the fund. Community foundations accept gifts of cash and other assets typically with a minimum value of $5,000.

Donors to community foundations generally have the option to contribute to any of at least three different types of funds:

1. **Unrestricted Fund:** The community foundation has complete discretion to make grants as it sees fit.
2. **Field of Interest Fund:** The community foundation allows the donor to designate special interest areas to receive grants such as the environment, arts, education or health. The community foundation makes discretionary grants to charities serving these fields of interest.
3. **Donor-Advised Fund:** The donor may recommend that grants be made in specific amounts to specific qualified charities from funds contributed by the donor. A donor-advised fund at a community foundation is an alternative to a private foundation, by allowing the donor to come under the tax and accounting

umbrella of a public charity. Those who want to be actively involved in grant making may designate this type of fund. In effect, the donor becomes an advisor. The community foundation, however, has final authority as to whether the donor's recommendation is approved. Contributions to community foundations are advised when a donor desires to have input as to the selection of charities in a specific geographic area.

Donor-Advised Funds

Community foundations are not the only charitable organization that offers the flexibility of a donor-advised fund. A number of national financial institutions have established public charities that offer donor-advised funds. As with the community foundation, the donor-advised funds associated with national financial institutions allow the donor to make an irrevocable gift to the fund, secure a tax deduction for the value of the contribution in the year of the gift, and yet take years to make grants. Donors enjoy having accounts named after their families and the simplification of having grants forwarded by the fund upon their request. The donor receives periodic statements concerning the value of the account and grants paid from it.

> Most donor-advised funds only accept gifts of liquid assets such as cash or securities. If a donor contributes appreciated stock (that has been owned for longer than a year) he gets an income tax deduction for the full fair market value of the stock and also avoids any capital gains tax on the appreciation.

Although contributions to the fund must be managed by the fund, the donor does become an advisor as to the amount and timing of grants from the donor's account. Grants are restricted to go only to qualified charities and must be consistent with the guidelines established by the board of directors of the donor-advised fund.

Donor-advised funds offered by national financial institutions differ from those offered by community foundations in two important aspects. First, the financial institutions impose few, if any, geographic limitations on the recipients of the grants. Second, they do not have in-house expertise relating to the charitable needs within local communities.

> One of the largest public charities in the country is a financial institution's donor-advised fund. In 2001 it had assets of about $2.5 billion and over 20,000 donors.

Typical donor-advised funds permit the donor to establish his own named fund (i.e., The Jones Fund) in the form of an account registered with the financial institution. The donor recommends the qualified charity and how much it should receive. Normally, the fund would have a $250 minimum gift amount. The donor-advised fund, has the legal right to reject recommendations.

Minimum initial contributions range from $10,000 to $50,000 with additional contributions made in smaller amounts. All administration is handled by the fund and any growth of the fund is tax free. Since the balance in the fund is hopefully growing on a tax free basis, this would perhaps result in a larger amount given to charity although the full amount of the tax deduction cannot be increased. There are management fees to be paid with such funds and they should be discussed carefully before using the services of any fund sponsored by a financial institution.

Donor-advised funds are appropriate for those who support multiple charities and like the idea of using a single fund to make all their grants. These funds are also appropriate for those who want to support charities without regard to geographic limitations and would like to make charitable contributions now for income tax purposes, but want to have the option to consider which charities should receive the amount contributed, and control the timing of the gifts.

> One advantage of the donor-advised fund over the private foundation is that tax deductions are limited to 30% of the donor's contribution base for contributions to private foundations, whereas contributions to a donor-advised fund qualify for an income tax deduction of up to 50% of the donor's contribution base.

Compared to private foundations, donor-advised funds have a number of advantages:

1. There are no startup fees for donor-advised funds, while the startup fees and administrative expenses of a private foundation can be significant.
2. There are no annual requirements for distributions from donor-advised funds. Private foundations are required to distribute 5% of the net asset value of the foundation each year.
3. Excise taxes of approximately 2% of annual income are required to be paid by private foundations; no such requirement is necessary for donor-advised funds.
4. The tax return for a private foundation is a public record (form PF-990) while donors may choose to remain anonymous as to the recipient of any grants made from their donor-advised fund.

Charitable Estate Planning with IRAs & Qualified Retirement Plans

There are a number of significant charitable estate planning opportunities based on the latest changes in the tax law regarding IRAs and qualified retirement plans. (*Please review Chapter 6 for a discussion of charitable estate planning with Qualified Retirement Plans and IRAs.*)

Summary

We have purposely left the material regarding charitable estate planning to be the final chapter of this book. Although we have considered the legal and technical aspects, such as what is a gift and what is a charity, the more important consideration is transferring your values to succeeding generations. The combination of tax benefits and the many strategies available to help others have a better life make charitable estate planning a particularly exciting pursuit.

About the Author

Mark L. James, M.B.A., J.D., LL.M. (tax) is an "of counsel" attorney with Hartman, Underhill and Brubaker LLP, a Lancaster County law firm. He is a graduate of Grove City College where he received his B.A. He received his M.B.A. from Michigan State University. His law degree was earned from the Regent University School of Law in Virginia Beach, VA (where he currently serves as a member of the board of trustees). He continued his law studies at the College of William and Mary, Marshall-Wythe School of Law, graduating with a Master of Laws in Taxation (LL.M.). Prior to law school, Mr. James was a financial advisor with a Wall Street brokerage firm. He has also served as a planned giving representative with an international non-profit organization where he raised millions of dollars in deferred gifts using charitable estate planning strategies. His law practice is concentrated in the areas of estate planning, estate and trust administration, and business law.

Mr. James has developed, written and presented numerous continuing education courses that have been approved by the Pennsylvania Insurance Department for continuing education credits as well as additional courses accepted by the Certified Financial Planner Board of Standards for continuing education credits.

Mr. James' professional affiliations include membership in the Pennsylvania and Lancaster County Bar Associations, the National Academy of Elder Law Attorneys, National Association of Estate Planners and Councils, Christian Legal Society and the Christian Stewardship Association. Mr. James is also registered by the Pennsylvania Insurance Department as a continuing education instructor and a life member of both the *National Registry of Who's Who* (published in 1999 edition) and *Who's Who in U.S. Writers, Editors & Poets* (published in 2002 edition). Mr. James lectures frequently on subjects within his area of expertise for a variety of professional and civic organizations including financial and estate planning professionals, non-profit organizations, colleges and retirement communities.

Mr. James can be contacted by writing or calling:

Barron Publishing Co.
Post Office Box 5039
Lancaster, Pennsylvania 17606
717 399-8112
e-mail: markj@barronpublishing.com

The Confidential Estate Planning Questionnaire

To do an effective job for you, we need reliable information about you and your assets, your family, and your desires. This questionnaire has been designed to be quickly and easily completed, and will provide both of us with a convenient record of information regarding your current estate.

When answering questions, specific amounts and complete answers are not necessary. Approximate information and estimates are satisfactory. During our conference, we will review this questionnaire together. Any points which may need further investigation can be discussed then.

With the facts gathered on the questionnaire, it will be possible to create a will or living trust to transfer your assets according to your wishes.

Your answers to this questionnaire will be held in strict confidence and no information will be given to anyone without your permission.

Please answer the questions with care and bring the questionnaire with you to your initial estate planning visit.

Date: ______________

Family Information

Client

NAME ____________________

BIRTH DATE ____________ SOCIAL SECURITY NO. ____________

HOME ADDRESS ____________________

CITY ____________ STATE ____________ ZIP ____________

TOWNSHIP/BOROUGH/COUNTY ____________________

TELEPHONE NO. ( ) ____________________

PLACE OF BIRTH ____________ CITIZENSHIP ____________

PREVIOUSLY MARRIED? ____________________

HOW TERMINATED ____________ TERMINATION DATE ____________

OCCUPATION ____________ EMPLOYER ____________

BUSINESS ADDRESS ____________________

CITY ____________ STATE ____________ ZIP ____________

BUSINESS TELEPHONE NO. ( ) ____________________

Spouse (if applicable)

NAME ____________________

BIRTH DATE ____________ SOCIAL SECURITY NO. ____________

HOME ADDRESS ____________________

CITY ____________ STATE ____________ ZIP ____________

TOWNSHIP/BOROUGH/COUNTY ____________________

TELEPHONE NO. ( ) ____________________

PLACE OF BIRTH ____________ CITIZENSHIP ____________

PREVIOUSLY MARRIED? ____________________

HOW TERMINATED ____________ TERMINATION DATE ____________

OCCUPATION ____________ EMPLOYER ____________

BUSINESS ADDRESS ____________________

CITY ____________ STATE ____________ ZIP ____________

BUSINESS TELEPHONE NO. ( ) ____________________

Profile of Your Children

Name of Child	From Which Marriage*	Age	Street, City, State & Zip of Residence	Marital Status	Number of Children For Child

** Use: Y = Child of this marriage H = Husband's previous marriage W = Wife's previous marriage*

Current Estate Profile	Yes	No
1. Does any family member have significant long-term health problems or other special needs?		
2. Do you now (or do you expect to) support anyone other than a child, such as a parent?		
3. Have you lived in any states other than Pennsylvania during your marriage?		
4. Do you and your spouse have a pre-nuptial agreement?		
5. Do you (or your spouse) expect a significant inheritance?		
6. Have you (or your spouse) created any trusts?		
7. Are you (or your spouse) a beneficiary of any trusts?		
8. Have you (or your spouse) ever filed a federal gift tax return?		
9. Do you (and your spouse) have a durable power of attorney?		
10. Do you (and your spouse) have a will or living trust?		
11. Do you (and your spouse) have a living will?		
12. Would you like to discuss a gift program to your children, or a trust for their benefit?		
13. Do you have any assets located in other states?		

Estate Asset Summary

	Asset	Client Owns	Spouse Owns	Jointly Owned
A.	Cash, Bank Accounts, Money Market Funds & CDs	$	$	$
B.	Money Owed to You			
C.	Bonds, Bond Funds & Treasury Bills			
D.	Stocks and Mutual Funds			
E.	Personal Residence (Today's Market Value)			
F.	Second Home (Today's Market Value)			
G.	Total of Other Real Estate (Today's Market Value)			
H.	Closely-Held Business Interests and/or Farm			
I.	Retirement Plans (including IRAs)			
J.	Interests in Estates and Trusts			
K.	Life Insurance (Face Value)			
L.	Automobiles			
M.	Household Furnishings & Personal Assets			
N.	Other Assets (such as Annuities)			
	Totals			

Please use your best estimate of these values in the applicable column.

Liabilities

Who Owes?*	To Whom Owed	Nature of Debt**	Current Balance

**Use: H = Husband W = Wife JT = Joint* ***Such as Bills, Mortgages, Notes Payable, etc.*

Distribution of Your Assets

	Distribution of Your Assets	Yes	No
1.	If Husband dies before Wife, 100% of estate to go to Wife?		
2.	If Wife dies before Husband, 100% of estate to go to Husband?		
3.	If Husband and Wife are both deceased, 100% of estate to go to all children equally?		

4. If any of the above answers are "No," list the names of your children, church, charity or others and the percentage (%) of your estate you desire to give to each. Alternatively, note the specific amount of cash or other assets you want to give to certain people or charities.

   Name Percentage

   1. ______________________________
   2. ______________________________
   3. ______________________________

5. If you and your spouse die prematurely, at what age do you want your children (or your grandchildren if both of their parents die prematurely) to receive your estate? Until this age, the trustee will take care of their financial needs. If no age is specified, they will receive 100% at age 18.

   ____% at age ____ ____% at age ____ Balance at age ____

6. If one of your children dies before you, that child's share to go to:

   1. ___ His/Her Children 2. ___ Your Other Living Children 3. ___ Your Deceased Child's Spouse

7. If none of your descendants are living at the time of your death, who do you want to receive your assets, such as extended family, friends or charities? Please list amounts and/or percentages.

   Name Percentage

   1. ______________________________
   2. ______________________________
   3. ______________________________

List in order of preference the persons and/or institution (such as a bank or trust company) you wish to name as your executor. Name at least two if you do not name a bank. For married clients, Husband is usually named first for Wife, and Wife is usually named first as executor for Husband, and each would then name someone else as an Alternate.

As Husband, I desire to name my wife as my executor. _____ Yes _____ No
As Wife, I desire to name my husband as my executor. _____ Yes _____ No

How should Executors #1 and #2 serve? ☐ Jointly ☐ First #1, Then #2

Executor of Your Estate

Name	Relationship	Address	City, State & Zip
1.			
2.			

If any of your children are minors (under 18), please indicate your first and second choices for guardians for them if something should happen to the two of you. (Please name two choices – your first choice and an Alternate.)

Guardians for Your Minor Children

Name	Relationship	Address	City, State & Zip
1.			
2.			

List in order of preference the persons and/or bank you wish to name as trustee for minor children or others. (If you do not name a bank, please name at least two choices – your first choice and an Alternate.)

How should Executors #1 and #2 serve? ☐ Jointly ☐ First #1, Then #2

Trustee of Trusts You Create in Your Will

Name	Relationship	Address	City, State & Zip
1.			
2.			

Original Trustee(s): You will be the initial trustee(s) unless you designate otherwise. **Successor Trustee(s):** At your death or disability, your back-ups will manage your trust. Your back-up trustee can be your adult children, financial advisor, trusted friend, bank and/or a trust company. If you select an individual, you should name a second choice in case your first is unable to serve.

Who Will Manage Your Revocable Living Trust?

Name	Relationship	Address	City, State & Zip
1.			
2.			

The Living Will Declaration

I, ____________________, being of sound mind, willfully and voluntarily make this declaration to be followed if I become incompetent. This declaration reflects my firm and settled commitment to refuse life-sustaining treatment under the circumstances indicated below.

I direct my attending physician to withhold or withdraw life-sustaining treatment that serves only to prolong the process of my dying, if I should be in a terminal condition or in a state of permanent unconsciousness.

I direct that treatment be limited to measures to keep me comfortable and to relieve pain, including any pain that might occur by withholding or withdrawing life-sustaining treatment.

In addition, if I am in the condition described above, I feel especially strong about the following forms of treatment:

I (__) do (__) do not want cardiac resuscitation.

I (__) do (__) do not want mechanical respiration.

I (__) do (__) do not want tube feeding or any other artificial or invasive form of nutrition (food) or hydration (water).

I (__) do (__) do not want blood or blood products.

I (__) do (__) do not want any form of surgery or invasive diagnostic tests.

I (__) do (__) do not want kidney dialysis.

I (__) do (__) do not want antibiotics.

I realize that if I do not specifically indicate my preference regarding any of the forms of treatment listed above, I may receive that form of treatment.

Other Instructions

I (__) do (__) do not want to designate another person as my surrogate to make medical treatment decisions for me if I should be incompetent and in a terminal condition or in a state of permanent unconsciousness. Name and address of surrogate:

Name: ____

Address: ____

Names of substitute surrogates (if surrogate designated above is unable to serve):

Name: ____

Address: ____

I (__) do (__) do not want to make an anatomical gift of all or part of my body, subject to the following limitations, if any: ______________________

I made this declaration on the ____ day of __________, 200__.

Declarant's signature: ________________________________

Declarant's address: _________________________________

The declarant or the person on behalf of and at the direction of the declarant knowingly and voluntarily signed this writing by signature or mark in my presence.

Witness's signature:__________________________________

Witness's address: ___________________________________

Witness's signature:__________________________________

Witness's address: ___________________________________

Tax without Credit Shelter Trust

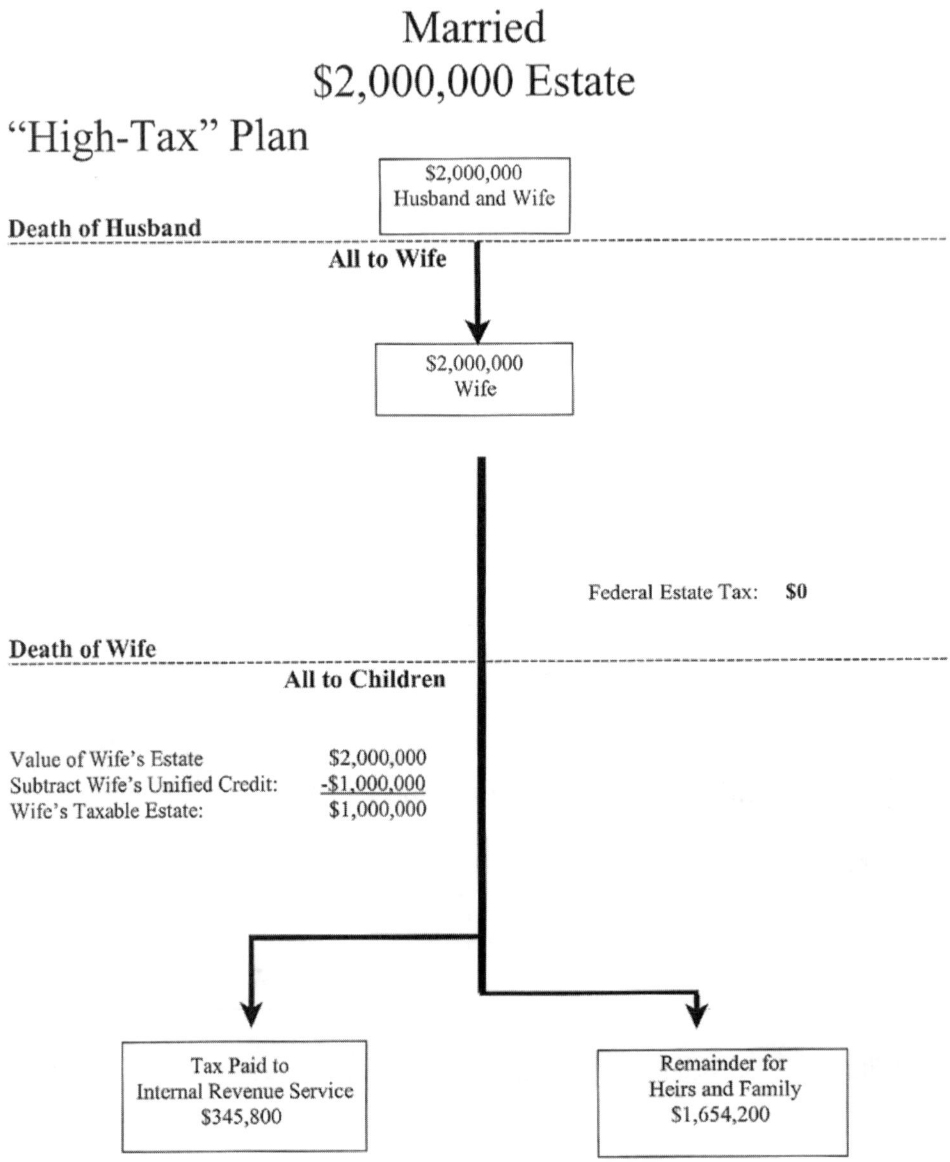

Tax with Credit Shelter Trust

Married
$2,000,000 Estate

Basic Tax-Saving Plan

$2,000,000
Husband and Wife

Death of Husband

All to Wife

$1,000,000
Wife

$1,000,000
Credit Shelter Trust

① Pour $1,000,000 of Husband's Estate into a Credit Shelter Trust for benefit of Wife.

- All Income goes to Wife.
- Wife receives $5,000 or 5% of Principal, whichever is greater each year.
- Wife can "invade" principal up to the entire amount for health, education, or support needs.

Federal Estate Tax: $0

② Balance goes outright to Wife.

Death of Wife

All to Children

Value of Wife's Estate:	$1,000,000
Subtract Wife's Unified Credit:	-$1,000,000
Wife's Taxable Estate:	**$0**

$1,000,000 to Heirs

Entire amount in Credit Shelter Trust is not included in Wife's Estate, so it passes tax-free to the children.

$1,000,000 to Heirs

Internal Revenue Service
$0

Heirs and Family
$2,000,000

Sample Crummey Letter

Timothy J. Jones, Trustee
The Bob and Shirley Jones Irrevocable Trust

Mr. Jim Jones
Philadelphia, PA

Re: Trustee's Notice to Beneficiary of Right of Withdrawal

Dear Jim:

On January 22, 2002, a gift of $22,000.00 was made to the Bob and Shirley Jones Irrevocable Trust.

This is to inform you that pursuant to the trust agreement, you have a legal right to withdraw your proportionate share of this contribution to the trust.

The amount of your proportionate share is $11,000.00. If you wish to make this withdrawal, you must do so within 30 days after receipt of the gift by me as trustee. If you decide not to make this withdrawal, you have legally waived your right to do so, and your share will remain in the trust, subject to control and discretion of the trustee.

This is a non-cumulative right, which means you cannot withdraw funds at any later date if you fail to withdraw your share of the current contribution to the trust at this time.

Please acknowledge the fact that you have received this notice by signing your name below, and returning this entire notice to me at the address above. Please contact me if you have any questions regarding this notice.

Sincerely,

Timothy J. Jones,
Trustee

I acknowledge that I have received this notice.

Signature of Beneficiary ______________________________ Date________________

The Technical Advisory Board & Their Professional Designations

Hopefully, after reading this book you have a grasp of the complexity of the world of estate planning. Not only is the subject matter broad in scope, but it is also constantly changing. Throughout this book I have emphasized the team approach to estate planning. As the author, I have used the team approach in writing this book. The following members of my Technical Advisory Board selflessly and voluntarily spent many hours reviewing various manuscripts of the book for technical accuracy. The depth and accuracy of the subject matter presented is due in a significant measure to the assistance of these generous professionals. Any errors are solely mine and are to be no reflection upon these advisors.

You will notice that after each advisor's name in the following directory, there is a series of letters. Indeed, with just over forty Technical Advisory Board Members, there are twenty different combinations of letters. These letters represent educational and professional qualifications. These professional designations and academic degrees indicate that the professional advisor has achieved certain educational experience and qualifications.

Following this list of advisors is an explanation of the meaning of their professional and acedemic designations.

Brandon L. Aumiller, LUTCF, CSA
Aumiller & Associates
6223 Old US Hwy. 322
Milroy, PA 17063
717-667-6501
braumiller@acsworld.net

Martyn S. Babitz, ESQ
Vice President, Senior Estate Planner
Director of Charitable Planning
PNC Advisors
1600 Market Street
Philadelphia, PA 19103
215-585-8776
martyn.babitz@pncbank.com

Robert A. Bacine, LL.M. (tax) ESQ
Flamm, Boroff & Bacine, PC
Attorneys at Law
925 Harvest Drive, Suite 220
Blue Bell, PA 19422
215-239-6003
rabacine@flammlaw.com

Charles Bauman
Executive Director
Friendship Community
1149 East Oregon Road
Lititz, PA 17543
717-656-2466
charlesbauman@friendship-comm.org

Thomas M. Brinker, Jr. CPA/PFS, AEP
Assoc. Professor of Accounting
Arcadia University
450 S. Easton Road
Glenside, PA 19038
215-572-4039
brinker@arcadia.edu

Carl L. Brubaker
Sr. Vice President, Trust and Investment Services
The Ephrata National Bank
31 East Main Street
Ephrata, PA 17522
717-733-6576
cbrubaker@ephratanationalbank.com

Gary L. Bukowski, CFRE
Vice Pres. for Institutional Advancement
Mercyhurst College
501 East 38th Street
Erie, PA 16546
814-824-2246
gbukowsk@mercyhurst.edu

Edward P. Carey, ESQ
Attorney at Law
3 Gateway Center, Suite 1460
Pittsburgh, PA 15222
412-391-7445
epcarey@sgi.net

Robert Clofine, ESQ
Certified as an Elder Law Attorney
by the National Elder Law Foundation
120 Pine Grove Commons
York, PA 17403
717-747-5995
clofine@estateattorney.com

Peter H. Craig, CLU, ChFC, AEP
Delaware Valley Financial Group
2540 Renaissance Blvd.
King of Prussia, PA 19406
484-322-4400
pcraig@dvfg.com

Charles A. DeBow, Jr., CLU, ChFC, AEP
2101 Welsh Road
Dresher, PA 19025
215-784-2007
charleydebow@msn.com

Stephen E. DiNovis, ESQ
Executive Vice President
Susquehanna Trust & Investment Co.
24 North Cedar Street
Lititz, PA 17543
717-626-4721
sedin@ffb.com

Sarah Young Fisher, ChFC, CFP, CFSC, EA
Fisher Advisers, Inc.
350 Highland Drive, C-160
Mountville, PA 17554
717-285-4008
sarahyoungfisher@aol.com

Stephen H. Frishberg, LL.M. (tax), CPA
Flamm, Boroff & Bacine, PC
Attorneys at Law
925 Harvest Drive, Suite 220
Blue Bell, PA 19422
215-239-6005
shfrishberg@flammlaw.com

Michele J. Garman, CFP
Vice President, Senior Trust Advisor
Wachovia Bank
100 North Queen Street
Lancaster, PA 17604
717-291-3616
michele.garmanl@firstunion.com

Wayne R. Gongaware, LUTCF, FIC
Aid Association for Lutherans
119B North Broad Street
Lititz, PA 17543
717-625-2330
wayne_gongaware@aol.org

William B. Henry, J.D., CFP
Edward Jones Investments
213 N. Main Street
Coudersport, PA 16915
814-274-2209
wbhenry@penn.com

Jack J. Hetherington, ESQ
Certified as an Elder Law Attorney
by the National Elder Law Foundation
Corr, Stevens & Fenningham
York Road (Route 263) and Bristol Road
Warminster, PA 18974
215-443-5443
jjh@corrlaw.com

H. Valentine Holz II, ESQ
The Holz Law Firm
4506 Miller Avenue
Erie, PA 16509
814-868-3900
holzlaw@thesolutionsfirm.net

John F. Keene, Jr., LUTCF
Planned Futures
711 Washington Blvd. Suite 200
Williamsport, PA 17701
570-322-8407
jfkinvest@sufcom.net

Kurt H. Kohler, CFP, LUTCF, CPA/PFS
Aid Association for Lutherans
11 Estates Drive
Reading, PA 19606
610-779-2016
kurtkohler@aal.org

Joseph T. Lee, LUTCF
Keys Insurance Agency, Inc.
551 North Laurel Street
Hazleton, PA 18201
570-455-9393
beppolee@hotmail.com

Steven T. Lees, ESQ, CFSC
Vice President & Trust Officer
First Nat'l. Bank & Trust Co. of Newtown
40 South State Street
Newtown, PA 18940
215-968-4872
stlees@fnbn.com

C. Kenneth Leith, CLU, ChFC, AEP
Leith Group
531 E. Lancaster Avenue
Wayne, PA 19087
610-687-5050
leithgroup@aol.com

Steven Leshner, MBA, CLU, ChFC, AEP
Commonwealth Consulting Group, Inc.
115 West Avenue, Suite 115
Jenkintown, PA 19046
215-884-2600
info@tccgroup.com

Jeffrey A. Marshall, ESQ
Certified as an Elder Law Attorney
by the National Elder Law Foundation
Marshall & Associates
303 Allegheny St.
Jersey Shore, PA 17740
570-398-7603
jmarshall@paelderlaw.com

Julian A. Marturano, CLU, ChFC, LUTCF
The MONY Group
4020 Route 130
Irwin, PA 15642
724-744-7400
JAY-Marturano@mony.com

Robb McKinney, CFS
McKinney Financial Advisors
399 Pittsburgh Road
Butler, PA 16002
724-586-9099
mckfinad@zbzoom.net

Joyce K. Moore, ChFC, LUTCF
Joyce Moore Financial Services
P.O. Box 175
Macungie, PA 18062
610-966-6127
joyce@jmfs.com

Michael D. Novak, CFP
Master's Financial Associates, Inc.
32-D East Roseville Road
Lancaster, PA 17601
717-581-1323
mnovak@mastersfinancial.com

Thomas J. Pappalardo
Vice Pres. for Institutional Advancement
Grove City College
100 Campus Drive
Grove City, PA 16127
724-458-2155
tjpappalardo@gcc.edu

Francis A. Procaccini, CLU, ChFC, AEP
Creative Planning Solutions
370 Southpointe Blvd., Suite 200
Canonsburg, PA 15317
724-743-6127
faprocaccini@lnc.com

John G. Richter, CFP, AEP, MT, EA
Montgomery, McCracken,Walker,
Rhoades
Attorneys at Law
123 S. Broad St., 25th Floor
Philadelphia, PA 19109
215-772-7404
jrichter@mmwr.com

Heidi J. Schellenger
Director of Land Preservation
Lancaster Farmland Trust
128 E. Marion Street
Lancaster, PA 17602
717-293-0707
heidi@savelancasterfarms.org

John J. Schneider, ESQ, AEP
Founding Member, National Network
of Estate Planning Attorneys
Weinstein, Schneider, Kannebecker
104 West High Street
Milford, PA 18337
717-296-6471
dschneider@mercurylink.net

Nancy Neff Solnick, ESQ
Certified as an Elder Law Attorney
by the National Elder Law Foundation
High, Swartz, Roberts & Seidel, LLP
40 E. Airy Street
Norristown, PA 19404
610-275-0700
nsolnick@highswartz.com

David Logan Steele, CTFA, AEP
Vice President, Senior Trust Officer
Jonestown Bank & Trust Company
421 East Penn Avenue
Cleona, PA 17042
717-279-8020
dls@jonestownbank.com

David B. Stork, ESQ
Vice Pres. Private Wealth Management
Investors Trust Company
2201 Ridgewood Road, Suite 180
Wyomissing, PA 19610
1-800-826-5534
dbstork@investorstrustco.com

Samuel T. Swansen, ESQ
Member, National Network
of Estate Planning Attorneys
610 Sentry Parkway, Suite 220
Blue Bell, PA 19422
610-834-9810
sam@samswansen.com

Michael D. Wiggins, MBA
Vice President - Wealth Management
Fulton Financial Advisors
One Penn Square
Lancaster, PA 17602
717-291-2554
mwiggins@fultonfinancialadvisors.com

Robert B. Williams, ESQ, AEP
Fellow of the American College of
Trusts and Estates Counsel
Williams Coulson
Two Chatham Center, 15th Floor
Pittsburgh, PA 15219
412-454-0222
williams@williamscoulson.com

Wayne C. Yoder, FIC, LUTCF
Lutheran Brotherhood
7306 New Berwick Hwy.
Bloomsburg, PA 17815
570-752-8884
waynec@bwkip.com

The following is a brief description of the professional and academic qualifications of the technical advisors and a note about the organization that confers the designation.

AEP - Accredited Estate Planner. A professional designation awarded by the National Association of Estate Planners and Councils. This designation is for estate planning practitioners who complete examination requirements and meet continuing education requirements. There are about 1200 members who hold this designation. The National Association of Estate Planners & Councils can be contacted at 270 S. Bryn Mawr Avenue, Bryn Mawr, PA 19010-2195, phone 610-526-1389, website - www.naepc.org.

CELA - Certified Elder Law Attorney. Attorneys with a CELA designation have been certified as an elder law attorney by The National Elder Law Foundation (NELF). To achieve this certification the Elder Law attorney must practice for at least five years and have an in-depth knowledge of the legal issues that impact the elderly. The NELF Certification process is approved by the American Bar Association and requires the attorney to complete a comprehensive examination. The National Elder Law Foundation can be contacted at 1604 North Country Club Road, Tucson, AZ 85716. Phone 520-881-1076, website - webmaster@nelf.org

CFP - Certified Financial Planner. The individual holding this designation has completed the Certified Financial Board of Standards academic certification requirements. More then 36,000 individuals use the CFP certification mark. Certified Financial Planner Board of Standards can be contacted at 1700 Broadway, Suite 2100, Denver, CO, 80290-2101. Phone 303-830-7500, website - www.CPF-Board.org

CFRE - Certified Fund Raising Executive. This designation is conferred on qualifying fundraising executives after five years of experience. It requires an application and a written examination. The CFRE Program is governed by the CFRE Professional Certification Board. The Program and the Board are administered in cooperation with a number of leading philanthropic associations.

CFS - Certified Fund Specialist. This designation is awarded to those who have completed a study course and examination. More than 10,000 people have this designation awarded by the Institute of Business and Finance. The Institute of Business and Finance can be contacted at 7911 Herschel Ave., Suite 201, La Jolla, CA 92037-4413. Phone 800-848-2029, website - www.icfs.com

CFSC - Certified Financial Services Counselor. This designation is obtained through attending the American Banker's Association's (ABA) National Graduate Trust School (Northwest University) in Illinois. Contact the American Banker's Association at 1120 Connecticut Avenue, NW, Washington, DC 20036. Phone 800-338-0626, website - www.aba.com

ChFC - Chartered Financial Consultant. One holding this designation has completed an educational program offered by the American College. In addition to examinations, the holder of this designation must meet experience and ethical standards and complete continuing education courses. Over 32,000 professional advisors have received this designation. The American College can be contacted at 270 S. Bryn Mawr Avenue, Bryn Mawr, PA 19010. Phone 610-526-1000, website - www.amercoll.edu .

CLU - Chartered Life Underwriter. A designation conferred upon those who have completed an educational program offered by the American College. This individual has also met experience and ethical standards and is required to complete continuing education. Approximately 85,000 have received the CLU designation. See Chartered Financial Consultant for contact information at the American College.

CPA - Certified Public Accountant. This individual has met academic qualifications such as Bachelors or Masters degree in accounting and has passed a series of state certifying examinations and meets experience qualifications in the area of public accounting.

CPA/PFS - Personal Financial Specialist. About 2500 CPAs have acquired this designation. Those holding the PFS designation must be existing CPAs who have experience in financial planning and pass an examination. The CPA/PFS is awarded by the American Institute of Certified Public Accountants. AICPA can be contacted at American Institute of Certified Public Accountants, Personal Financial Planning Division, 1211 Avenue of the Americas, New York, NY, 10036-8775. Phone 888-777-7077, website - www.aicpa.org

CSA - Certified Senior Advisor. The Society of Certified Senior Advisors grants the Certified Senior Advisor designation. It is an educational organization that provides training on senior issues to professionals who work with seniors. There are over 3,000 holding this designation who are required to complete continuing education. The Society of Certified Senior Advisors can be contacted at 1777 South Bellaire Street, Suite 230, Denver, CO 80222. Phone 1-800-653-1785, website - www.society-csa.com.

CTFA - Certified Trust and Financial Advisor. The American Institute of Banking awards this designation to those who meet educational requirements and pass extensive examinations in the areas of tax law, investments, personal finance and fiduciary responsibilities. The American Institute of Banking can be contacted at 80 Maiden Lane, New York City, NY, 10036. Phone 212-480-3200, website - www.aibny.edu

EA - Enrolled Agent. A designation given by the Internal Revenue Service to enable individuals to represent others before the IRS.

ESQ - Esquire. This is a popular designation given to licensed attorneys who are actively engaged in the practice of law.

FIC - Fraternal Insurance Counselor. This designation is conferred by the Fraternal Field Managers' Association on those who successfully complete educational requirements and meet required qualifications. Contact the National Fraternal Congress of America at 1240 Iroquois Drive - Suite 300, Naperville, IL 60563. Website - www.nfcanet.org.

J.D. - Juris Doctor. The academic degree awarded to one who has completed a three-year study of law. The initials J.D. are usually used instead of the letters "ESQ." to designate an attorney who has graduated from law school but who is not actively engaged in the practice of law.

LL.M. (tax) - Master of Laws in Taxation. An academic degree awarded to attorneys who have completed law school and have, in addition, completed further academic work at a law school to achieve a second law degree with a concentration in tax law.

LUTCF - Life Underwriter Training Council Fellow. This designation is awarded to persons in the life insurance industry who have completed courses relating to life and health insurance. The designation is conferred by the Life Underwriter Training Council. There are currently about 60,000 persons who have completed this program. Life Underwriting Training Council can be contacted at 7625 Wisconsin Avenue, Bethesda, MD 20814-3560. Phone 301-913-5882, website - www.lutc.org.

MBA - Master of Business Administration. An academic degree awarded to those who have completed a four-year undergraduate degree program and have continued on with further academic studies concentrated in areas related to business administration.

MT - Master of Taxation. An academic degree conferred upon those who have completed a four-year college degree and have continued on to post-graduate studies specializing in the area of taxation.

Glossary

AB Trust - A trust giving a surviving spouse a lifetime interest in assets of a deceased spouse. This trust is designed to save on estate taxes by giving a surviving spouse only the income from the assets of the first spouse to die. Also known as a "credit shelter trust" or "bypass trust."

Abatement - A reduction in the amount of a bequest under a will because the assets of the estate are insufficient to pay all debts, taxes, and bequests in full.

Ademption - The failure of a specific bequest of assets to be made, because the decedent did not own the assets at the time of death.

Adjusted Gross Estate - For federal estate tax purposes, the gross estate less debts, administration expenses, and losses during administration.

Administration - The process of settling a decedent's estate. The duties include valuing estate assets, filing tax returns and paying taxes, and distributing assets to heirs.

Administration Expenses - The expenses incurred during the administration of an estate. These include legal and accounting fees, appraisal fees, and distribution costs.

Administrator - Person or institution appointed by a court to represent an estate when there is no will. Also called a personal representative.

Advance Medical Directive - See "Living Will."

Advancement - A bequest made in a will, which is reduced because of gifts made to that person during lifetime.

Affidavit - A written statement made under oath before a notary public or authorized officer of the court.

Agent - The person given authority by one signing a power of attorney to transact business in his or her name.

Alternate Beneficiary - The person or organization named to receive assets if the primary beneficiary dies before the one naming the beneficiaries.

Alternate Valuation Date - The date six months after a decedent's death for federal estate tax purposes. The personal representative has the option of valuing estate assets as of the date of death or the alternate valuation date, if certain criteria are met.

Anatomical Gift - A gift of one or more body organs upon death.

Ancillary Administration - Administration of an estate in another state in addition to the state where the decedent lived. Typically required when the decedent owns real estate in another state.

Annual Exclusion Amount - The amount ($11,000 adjusted for inflation) one is permitted to give away to any other person each year without paying gift tax or filing a gift tax return. There is no limit on the number of people to whom gifts can be made each calendar year.

Annuity - A contractual right to receive a fixed sum of money at specific intervals either for life or for a minimum term of years.

Annuity Trust - One form of charitable remainder trust that pays a fixed amount to a person regularly. The amount paid is based on the value of a gift at the time the trust is established, age of donor, and interest rates.

Applicable Credit Amount - See "Lifetime Exclusion Amount."

Ascertainable Standard - The right of a surviving spouse serving as the trustee, to invade a credit shelter trust, without causing the trust's assets to be included in his or her estate. The power is limited to using trust assets for the spouse's "health, education, maintenance, and support."

Bargain Sale - The sale of assets for less than their current fair market value.

Basis - The amount paid to acquire an asset. The value is used to determine gain or loss for income tax purposes upon the asset's subsequent sale.

Beneficiary - The person or organization that receives assets from a will or trust after the death of the trust grantor. The word also refers to those who receive assets from an annuity, life insurance policy, or retirement plan.

Bequest - A gift left to a person or organization under a will or trust.

Buy-Sell Agreement - A contract between partners or shareholders of a corporation that determines the conditions and price for a buyout by one at the death or retirement of the other.

Bypass Trust - A trust for married couples that does not qualify for the unlimited estate tax marital deduction. Commonly referred to as the family trust, or B trust, or credit shelter trust. It is designed to use the lifetime exclusion amount of the first spouse to die.

Capital Gains Tax - Income tax on the gain from the sale of an asset. The amount taxed is calculated by subtracting tax basis from the sale price.

Certificate of Trust - A brief version of a trust that verifies the trust's existence, describes trustee's powers, and identifies the successor trustee.

Charitable Lead Trust - A trust in which a charity receives income for a certain period of time with the remainder passing to the donor's beneficiaries after a specified period of time.

Charitable Remainder Trust - A trust where the beneficiary receives income payments for lifetime or a term of years (not to exceed 20). Upon the beneficiary's death, assets remaining in the trust pass to a charitable organization.

Co-Trustees - Two or more individuals appointed to serve together to manage a trust's assets. A corporate trustee can also be a co-trustee.

Codicil - A legal document which changes or modifies the will.

Community Property States - States in which all assets acquired by either partner in a marriage are considered owned one half by each partner. Community property states are Arizona, California, Idaho, Louisiana, Nevada, New Mexico, Texas, Washington, and Wisconsin.

Conservation Easement - A permanent easement placed on real estate that prevents it from being developed into commercial real estate.

Contest of a Will - Legal action taken to change or prevent the distribution of assets as set forth in a decedent's will. The usual claims are that the decedent was incompetent when they signed their will or they were under the undue influence of another person.

Contingent Beneficiary - An alternate person or organization selected in case the primary beneficiary dies before the one naming beneficiaries.

Corporate Trustee - A bank trust department or trust company that specializes in managing trusts.

Corpus - Assets the grantor places in trust. Also known as the principal of a trust.

Credit Shelter Trust - A trust established under a will or living trust to take advantage of the lifetime exclusion amount of the first spouse to die. (Also known as a bypass trust or a B trust)

Crummey Power - The right held by the beneficiary of a trust to withdraw from the trust a portion of every contribution to the trust.

Custodian - The person named to manage a minor's assets under the Uniform Transfer to Minors Act.

Decedent - A person who has died.

Deed - A legal document by which one person transfers title to real estate to another person or persons.

Disclaimer - The refusal to accept assets one is entitled to receive. The disclaimed assets will be transferred to the next person as provided by a will or trust. Disclaimers must be completed within nine months of death.

Domicile - The state in which one has their permanent residence.

Donee - A person who receives a gift.

Donor - A person who makes a gift.

Durable Power of Attorney - A power of attorney which continues as a legal document even if the principal later becomes incapacitated.

Durable Power of Attorney for Health Care - A legal document that gives someone the authority to make health care decisions for the principal in the event he or she is unable to make them.

Elective Share - A portion of the estate that a surviving spouse is entitled to by law regardless of what the decedent's will states.

Escheat - Assets that go to a state government because there are no legal heirs to claim it.

Estate - Assets or property that one owns or has the rights to possess.

Estate Administration - The process of handling the affairs of decedent's estate.

Estate Planning - The process of developing a plan to provide for the tax effective and orderly distribution of an individual's assets at the time of death, or the management of their assets during lifetime if they become incapacitated.

Estate Tax - A tax imposed by the federal government and Pennsylvania on the right of a person to transfer assets at death. This transfer tax is applicable to estates valued over and above the "lifetime exclusion amount" which is $1,000,000 for 2002.

Executor - The person or institution appointed in a will to administer the estate, deal with the probate court, collect assets and distribute them as specified. Also known as the personal representative.

Fair Market Value - The value at which assets are included in the gross estate for federal estate tax purposes. The price at which assets would change hands between a willing buyer and a willing seller.

Family Limited Partnership - A type of partnership that provides asset protection and allows for management and control of assets by the general partners.

Fiduciary - A person or institution in a position of trust and responsibility. Examples are the executor of a will, trustee of a trust, or agent under a power of attorney.

Five and Five Powers - The right of a trust beneficiary to withdraw from the principal of a trust the greater of 5% of the value of the trust or $5,000 per year.

Funding a Trust - The process of transferring assets into a trust.

Generation-Skipping Transfer (GST) Tax - A tax assessed on gifts in excess of $1,060,000 (adjusted for inflation) to grandchildren, great-grandchildren, and others at least two generations below the individual making the gift.

Gift Tax - A federal tax imposed on gifts made while living. $11,000 (adjusted for inflation) per person per year is exempt from gift tax. See "annual exclusion amount."

Grantor - The person who establishes a trust. Also called the settlor or trustor.

Grantor Trust - A trust where income is taxable to the grantor because he or she retains substantial control over the trust assets or retains certain administrative powers. All trust values are included in grantor's estate for estate and inheritance tax purposes.

Gross Estate - The total value of assets left by the decedent. The amount required to be included in his or her estate for estate tax purposes.

Guardian - A person appointed by the court to have custody over the person or the assets (or both) of a minor or incapacitated person.

Guardian of the Estate - An individual or institution appointed by the court to manage the assets of a minor or an incapacitated person.

Guardian of the Person - An individual or institution appointed by the court to care for a minor or an incapacitated person.

Heir - One who receives the assets of a decedent by operation of law or by will or trust.

Holographic Will - A will that is completely handwritten.

Incapacity - The mental state of being unable to make decisions regarding management of one's own assets or medical needs.

Inheritance Tax - A tax on the heir of a decedent for assets inherited. Tax rates depend on the relationship of the heir to the decedent.

Inter Vivos Trust - A trust established during one's lifetime. Also called a living trust.

Intestacy Laws - State laws which control who will receive the assets of a person who dies without a will.

Intestate - A person who dies without a will; that person is said to have died intestate.

Irrevocable Trust - A trust that cannot be revoked, canceled or amended once it is established. The opposite of a revocable trust.

Issue - Direct descendants of an individual such as children, grandchildren and great-grandchildren.

Joint Ownership - Two or more persons owning the same asset.

Joint Tenants with Right of Survivorship - One way to take title to jointly owned assets. At the death of one joint owner, the surviving joint owner(s) automatically receive the deceased person's interest. (See also "tenants in common" and "tenants by the entirety.")

Lapse - The failure of a bequest in a will that occurs when the intended recipient dies before the testator.

Letters Testamentary - The document issued by the court authorizing the executor to discharge his responsibilities.

Life Estate - The right to use assets and receive income from them during one's lifetime. At death, that person's rights terminate.

Lifetime Exclusion Amount - The dollar value of assets that one can give to a non-spouse either during lifetime or at death free of estate taxes. For 2002, the dollar value is $1 million.

Limited Power of Attorney - A power of attorney that limits the agent's authority to certain actions.

Living Trust - A trust established by a person during his or her lifetime. If it is revocable, it can be amended or terminated anytime. The trust becomes irrevocable upon death.

Living Will - A document that states a person's wishes regarding certain types of medical treatment in the event of a terminal illness or coma.

Marital Deduction - A federal estate tax deduction for assets received by the deceased's spouse. Amount is unlimited if the surviving spouse is a U.S. citizen.

Marital Trust - A trust consisting of assets qualifying for the federal estate tax marital deduction.

Medicaid - Program funded by the federal and state government to pay medical costs of those who are financially unable to pay. Known as "medical assistance" in Pennsylvania.

Net Taxable Estate - The gross estate for federal estate tax purposes reduced by allowable deductions, credits, and charitable contributions.

Nonprobate Assets - Assets passing outside the administration of the probate estate. Examples include jointly held assets passing by right of survivorship and life insurance proceeds payable to a named beneficiary.

Orphan's Court - The division of the Pennsylvania Court of Common Pleas that is assigned to have jurisdiction over issues relating to probate, estates and guardianships.

Payable on Death - A designation for certificates of deposit and bank accounts which states that, upon the owner's death, the account is to be transferred to the named beneficiary.

Pennsylvania Uniform Transfer to Minors Act - See "Uniform Transfer to Minor's Act."

Per Capita - A method of distributing estate assets so that surviving descendants share equally regardless of generation.

Per Stirpes - A method of distributing estate assets so that the surviving descendants of a predeceased heir will receive only what their immediate ancestor would have received if he or she had been alive at the time of death.

Personal Representative - A person or institution administering an estate, as executor or administrator.

Pour-Over Will - A will used with a revocable living trust that "pours over" assets into a trust. Assets controlled by the will must go through probate before it goes into the trust.

Power of Attorney - A document that gives one person (the agent) authority to take legal action and sign the name of another person (the principal).

Pre-Nuptial Agreement - A contract signed by husband and wife before marriage that limits their asset rights in the future.

Principal - The person who signs a power of attorney and thereby gives the agent named therein the authority to act on his or her behalf.

Principal - The assets funding a trust. Trust principal is also known as corpus.

Probate - Procedure which validates a will. It also is used to refer to the administration process of an estate.

Probate Estate - The property and assets of the deceased, distributed under direction of the will.

Probate Assets - The assets that are distributed to heirs under the terms of a will. If there is no will, it passes under the intestacy laws.

Qualified Domestic Trust (Q-DOT) - A trust to which assets are transferred so that a spouse who is not a U.S. citizen will be entitled to claim the benefit of the unlimited marital deduction form the federal estate tax.

Qualified Terminal Interest Property (Q-TIP) Trust - A trust that requires a surviving spouse to receive all income, but which transfers assets to persons designated by the deceased after the death of the surviving spouse. The trust qualifies for the unlimited marital deduction from the federal estate tax.

Remainderman - The person entitled to receive the principal of a trust at the time the prior life estate terminates.

Residue - The portion of an estate that remains after all specific distributions have been made.

Revocable Trust - A trust that can be altered, amended, or revoked by the grantor during lifetime.

Settlor - The grantor or creator of a trust.

Spendthrift Clause - A clause in a trust document that protects assets in a trust from a beneficiary's creditors.

Springing Power of Attorney - A power of attorney that only gives the agent powers after a certain event occurs, such as the incapacity of the principal.

Standby Trust - An unfunded living trust executed with a durable power of attorney to which assets may be subsequently transferred.

Step-Up in Basis - The tax basis of appreciated assets held by a decedent "steps up" to fair market value on the date of death.

Successor Trustee - The individual or institution who takes over as trustee of a trust when the original trustee dies, becomes incapacitated, or resigns.

Taxable Estate - The portion of ones estate that is subject to federal and state taxes. Funeral and administrative expenses; debts (including certain unpaid taxes); charitable contributions, and the marital deduction all may be deducted from the gross estate to determine the taxable estate.

Tenancy by Entirety - Joint ownership of assets by husband and wife. Such assets may not be disposed of during life by either spouse without the other's consent. At one spouse's death, the assets are automatically transferred to the survivor.

Tenants-in-Common - A form of joint ownership in which the same assets are owned by two or more persons. At the death of one tenant-in-common, his share is controlled by his will. It does not automatically pass to the surviving tenants-in-common.

Testamentary Trust - A trust that is created under a will and takes effect only after the grantor's death.

Testator or Testatrix (female) - One who has created a will.

Totten Trust - Another term for a pay-on-death bank account.

Trust - A document whereby one individual (called the trustor, grantor or settlor), places assets under the management of another individual or institution (the trustee) for the benefit of a third person (the beneficiary).

Trustee - An individual or institution that administers a trust.

Uniform Transfer to Minors Act - A law that permits one to give a gift to a minor by giving the gift to a custodian who holds title to the assets for the benefit of the minor.

Unlimited Marital Deduction - A provision in the estate and gift tax law that allows a married person to leave unlimited assets to his or her spouse free of gift or estate tax.

Will - A written document with instructions for disposition of assets at death.

Index

Couldn't Someone You Know Benefit from Reading *ESTATE PLANNING SUCCESS™ FOR PENNSYLVANIA RESIDENTS?*

It makes a meaningful gift for your friends, family members, clients, and donors. Check with your local bookstore, which will be glad to order additional copies if they are sold out. Or, you can order directly by using this Quick Order Form.

How To Order More Books:

Mail: Complete this form and mail to:
BookMasters
P.O. Box 2139
Mansfield OH 44905
Make check payable to BookMasters.

Phone: Call toll free 1 (800) 247-6553 (Have your credit card ready.)

Fax: Complete this form and fax to 1 (419) 281-6883

E-mail: info@bookmasters.com

Internet: Visit us at www.barronpublishing.com and place your order on our web site.

Please rush me _______ copies of *Estate Planning Success™ for Pennsylvania Residents* at $34.95 each which includes the book, shipping and Pennsylvania sales tax. (Deduct $1.80 per book for books delivered outside of Pennsylvania.)

Name: ____

Address: ____

City: ____________________ State: ____________ Zipcode: __________

Telephone: ______________________________

e-mail: ______________________________

Method of Payment

☐ Check enclosed ☐ Mastercard

☐ Visa ☐ American Express

Account # ______________________ Exp. Date ____________

Signature ______________________

Quantity discounts are available. Please call or write for information.